Rethinking Advertising as Paratextual Communication

T0327406

For our family

Rethinking Advertising as Paratextual Communication

Chris Hackley

Professor of Marketing, Royal Holloway University of London, UK

Rungpaka Amy Hackley

Senior Lecturer in Marketing, Birkbeck University of London, UK

 Edward Elgar
PUBLISHING

Cheltenham, UK • Northampton, MA, USA

Published by
Edward Elgar Publishing Limited
The Lypiatts
15 Lansdown Road
Cheltenham
Glos GL50 2JA
UK

Edward Elgar Publishing, Inc.
William Pratt House
9 Dewey Court
Northampton
Massachusetts 01060
USA

Paperback edition 2023

A catalogue record for this book
is available from the British Library

Library of Congress Control Number: 2022932134

This book is available electronically in the **Elgar**online
Business subject collection
http://dx.doi.org/10.4337/9781800882621

ISBN 978 1 80088 261 4 (cased)
ISBN 978 1 80088 262 1 (eBook)
ISBN 978 1 0353 1213 9 (paperback)

Printed and bound by CPI Group (UK) Ltd, Croydon, CR0 4YY

Contents

1. Advertising as paratextual communication

INTRODUCTION

What do you think the following have in common? A best-selling book authored by a CGI meerkat; Nike Swooshes; the viral video 'You're more beautiful than you think'; hashtagged social media challenges; stuffed Kevin the Carrot toys; brands mentioned in influencer content; 'sponsored by' Facebook ads; online Tripadvisor reviews; the Michelin Guide; Red Bull's video coverage of cliff-diving competitions; an Apple laptop visible in the scene of a movie; posters in underground tube stations; high-street advertising billboards; TV channel brand 'idents' before the show titles, and sponsor's 'interstitials' placed after the titles;[1] Google search engine advertising; general media news stories about brand organisations; Amazon product reviews: clips on video sharing websites of GoPro users doing the rapids; hit music tracks in broadcast advertisements; and brand-produced short movies like BMW's The Hire series?

We will return to this question below, but, for now, we want to outline what this book is about and how it will progress. In what follows we will adapt a selection of ideas from literary theory to examine how they might change the way advertising is understood by students of advertising, by scholars, and by media and management professionals. The central organising idea we apply is the notion of the paratext, a secondary text that acts as a threshold through which we enter the primary text to which it refers. Our take on paratextuality and related concepts can perhaps be described as a poststructuralist twist on the work of French literary critic Gérard Genette,[2] aided and abetted by work in traditions of intertextuality from Kristeva and Barthes, building on Bakhtin's dialogism and Iser's reader-response theory. We also briefly consider semiotic perspectives on advertising in digital media, through approaches such as performative citationality.[3] Our goal, overall, is to apply simplified applications of these ideas in a practical and accessible revision of how advertising can be understood in the convergence era[4] as paratextual communication. In developing the argument of the book we try to follow where this idea leads for advertising and brand management practice, and for academic research into advertising.

THE COMMONALITY OF PARATEXTUAL ADVERTISING

So, to return to our opening question: all the examples above are, of course, examples of media content connected to marketing and/or advertising. You might well have encountered some of them. The price comparison website comparethemarket.com's CGI meerkats have been ubiquitous in UK media for more than a decade since they were invented as a handy way to increase the brand's visibility in search advertising. The meerkats have subsequently become an entire storyworld represented by books (ostensibly authored by the aforementioned meerkat), TV appearances, cuddly toys and much more.[5] You might also have seen the Kevin the Carrot brand character used to promote the supermarket Aldi in the UK in many epic UK TV ads. You could be one of the circa 70 million viewers who have seen cosmetics brand Dove's 2013 YouTube video 'You're More Beautiful Than You Think',[6] or one of the 100 million who have watched Volvo's (and Jean-Claude Van Damme's) The Epic Split,[7] a short movie advertising their trucks. You might even have watched one of the series of car chase-based short films funded by BMW and available on YouTube, such as their 2012 production directed by (no less) John Frankenheimer and starring Clive Owen, called Ambush,[8] in which the car ends up riddled with bullet holes, but somehow still running silkily. If there was a genre called white-knuckle advertising, this would be it.

They are also very different in their positioning on the promotional spectrum. The Michelin Guide, for example, is known as the archetype for content marketing, also called branded content, a burgeoning technique[9] of implicit advertising that features brands in, or in connection with, news, information and entertainment. The Michelin Guide had a subtle promotional motive when it was designed at the turn of the 20th century[10] to tempt French car drivers to venture further afield to try the latest exquisite restaurant, thus wearing out their car tyres more quickly. The Epic Split, Dove's viral movie 'Beautiful' and the BMW movies mentioned above are examples of branded video, while the meerkats Aleksandr, Sergai and Oleg,[11] along with their vegetable counterpart,

Kevin the Carrot,[12] are part of a long tradition of brand characters going back to the Pillsbury Doughboy from the 1960s, the PG Tips Chimps and Kellogg's Frosties's Tony the Tiger in the 1950s, and the Rice Crispies elves Snap, Crackle and Pop from the 1940s, deployed for their well-known ability to anthropomorphise the brand, cueing an emotional response from the consumer, and helping to make the brand easier to remember.[13] Advertising posters and billboards, often grouped together with ads on urban street furniture or bus stops as Out Of Home (OOH) advertising, and PR (Public Relations) initiatives designed to generate news coverage about brands, are both old school techniques, in contrast to influencer[14] and social media advertising which are part of the murky and hyperbolic world of digital promotion. Digital media have taken sponsorship to new places as video sharing platforms have extended audience reach for video clips of sponsored sports events to hundreds of millions, opening up opportunities for clips that have Red Bull, GoPro or Nike involved in some way. The ways in which consumers can take on the burden of advertising brands through UGC (User Generated Content) by posting their home-made GoPro film clips or acerbic restaurant reviews have also been enabled by many new digital platforms. As for brands in movies and TV shows, product placement is no longer a dirty secret in the entertainment industry and has long been noted in Victorian novels and stage plays[15] as well as being common in contemporary computer and video games and popular songs.[16]

So, as tactical or strategic promotional techniques the examples differ, unquestionably, and they also differ as genres of entertainment or information. But they also share a deep commonality. They represent a palpable shift in the logic of advertising practice, from explicit sales appeals to implicit publicity, and from traditional advertising, to media content[17] that is connected to a brand, explicitly, where branding is visible in the content, or implicitly, where the relationship between brand and content might be known but not stated. This dual shift does not apply to most search engine and social media advertising, which is avowedly sales oriented and simply constructed with a headline and a click-through link to the brand website. It applies to the other half[18] of annual global adspend, the bigger-budget areas of commissioned creative advertising and brand content. We can see this trend not only in the amount of strategic importance advertisers now give to implicit advertising in the form of, for example, sponsorship, brand placement and (of course) content advertising,[19] but also in the frequency with which traditional paid-for advertising deviates from the genre conventions of traditional advertising by failing to feature a sales proposition, or even by failing to prominently feature the brand, in favour of more oblique storytelling (we return to this theme below with the Nationwide bank 'Voices' campaign example). Most of the examples listed above are characterised by the implicit or by-the-way presence of the brand, as if it is incidental to the main purpose of the communication. Which it is, and it also isn't. What is more, many of these examples are positioned as originating from a source that is arms-length from or independent of the brand,[20] such as the Dove viral videos.[21] Their ostensible purpose as promotional communications, then, is confused by the lack of any sales pitch, any explicitly persuasive element in them, and in the case of arm's-length content, by an apparent wish to disavow ownership of the brand. We know, though, as a matter of common knowledge, that brands want us to buy them, and their presence in media content of whatever kind for whatever audience is intended or hoped to encourage audiences to do so. There is something odd, then, about the enormous presence in our media landscape of advertisements that appear not to satisfy the genre conventions of advertising. The pragmatics of this advertising-that-does-not-seem-to-behave-like-advertising can be confusing. Are we supposed to be persuaded to buy a BMW after we enjoy a clip of Ambush? Or are we allowed to simply enjoy the movie? And if so, how does that benefit BMW? Of the millions of viewers who enjoyed watching Jean-Claude Van Damme's eye-watering flexibility in Epic Split, how many bought a Volvo truck? How many of the sophisticated (and well-heeled) foodies who seek out Michelin starred restaurants make a point of buying only Michelin tyres for their cars? Are the big brands being super clever, or are they just throwing silly money at ad agencies, movie stars and Hollywood film producers because they like hanging out with them? Who benefits from such branded entertainment, and how?

In this book we hope to explain what's going on with the help of some ideas from literary theory. The most important of these is the idea that the kind of media content we have mentioned above, whether a 20-second TV advertisement, a viral video, a short movie, a piece of branded content or a billboard featuring a furry brand character, can be understood as a secondary or (in the term used by Gérard Genette in the context of literary works) a paratext, that refers to a primary text. For Genette, the paratext refers to the primary text of the literary work, the printed novel, poetry collection or libretto. In our adaptation of paratextuality we use the term to refer to any media content whatsoever that is connected to a brand, and the primary text to which it refers as the brand, a notional primary text.

The suggestion that advertisements can be understood as forms of paratext will be unsurprising to the many cultural, literary, film and TV scholars who have been using Genette's work to shed light on the dynamics of media content and audience reception. Such work[22] tends to focus on the promotional paratexts of movies, TV shows and other media brands. We want to establish the application of the idea of the paratext more widely to apply to any sector of brand in our own discipline of business and management, specifically the broad area of marketing, branding and advertising. Our treatment will take in all forms of advertising and brand communication, reflecting the seamless digital advertising environment as it is experienced by audiences. Our approach will move away from the disciplinary silos of the promotional mix and challenge the 100 years' old theories of persuasive communication that still dominate business school thinking on advertising. We hope to show that the idea of the paratext captures something of the kinetic, fluid and relational character of advertising and brand communication under digitisation, and we hope to use it to generate new insights into the role advertising plays in the audience experience, and in the management of brands. In the book we will refer to many works of research and scholarship that provide the foundations for the approach we take, but each chapter also provides numerous references to case examples, videos, trade press pieces and other resources that ground the ideas in a practical advertising context and illustrate the applications of the various theoretical perspectives. Our intention is to make the book accessible to practitioners and students, and persuasive to academics working in these and related fields of business, social, cultural and media studies.

THE IDEA OF PARATEXTUALITY

We should take the opportunity here to outline what we think we mean by a paratext before dealing in more detail with the topic as the book progresses. Genette's work[23] focused on literary paratexts as they occur in paper-bound works of poetry or prose. These paratexts take the form of footnotes, book and chapter titles, images, prefaces, forewords, cover blurbs and all the other literary paraphernalia that is included within the primary work (peritexts, in Genette's taxonomy), along with external paratexts (epitexts) such as advertisements for the book, published interviews with the author, the author's handwritten notes and first drafts, compilations, adaptations, parodies and any other external texts that refer to the primary work. Genette's insight was that these paratexts are not peripheral to the meaning of the primary text – rather, they act as thresholds through which the reader enters the text. Hence, they are far more important than often thought since they frame, inflect and sometimes change the meaning of the primary text. Indeed, for Genette, the primary text cannot exist without its paratexts.

There are those who will insist that the primary text has a special status and that paratexts are indeed mere periphera, regardless of the ways they might superficially influence casual opinion. *Little Women, The Gulag Archipelago, War and Peace* are great works that have a meaning that is essential to the work and is unconnected to their associated paratexts, or at least that is the view. We will discuss more of the hierarchical relation of primary to secondary text later in the book. For now, we will focus on the idea that Genette turned conventional literary wisdom on its head by showing that the meaning of a literary work is not given entirely by the text itself, but also by the paratexts that surround it and that, in a sense, bring the text into existence since they are the threshold through which audiences enter the text.

Genette acknowledged that his ideas could apply to other forms of social text besides paper-bound literary works and, as we note earlier, they have indeed been adapted extensively in media, film and television studies to understand, for example, how the layers of paratextual content that circulate around movies, such as posters and advertisements, trailers, star interviews, critics' reviews, fan fiction and internet comment (or UGC) impact on how a movie is interpreted and understood. To extend the idea into branding and advertising, we take the view that a brand paratext could be any media content that is connected to a brand, explicitly or implicitly. With that brief outline of the key idea, we will continue with an outline of the book and a discussion of advertising genres, before picking up again on Genette's ideas and their applicability (or otherwise) to our subject, in Chapter 2.

AN OUTLINE OF THE BOOK

Chapter 1 outlines the key ideas of the book. We have briefly sketched out Genette's approach to paratexts, but we must also explain a baseline assumption that we make about advertising practice. This is that, in spite of the differences between the countless sub-categories of advertising and brand communication that we encounter in our mediated and un-mediated lives, they share a fundamental unity. We feel that understanding these different categories of promotional media content as brand paratexts reveals their essential connectedness in a way that allows us to develop a more holistic approach to analysing the ways advertising, audiences and brands interact. We use a range of examples that show how the sub-categories of advertising are collapsing into each other under the influence of digital technology and because of concomitant changes in how audiences access, and engage with, media. We believe, overall, that understanding advertising as paratextual communication responds to an acute need to update the way advertising is conceived for the purposes of advertising agencies, brands, consumers, and students and scholars in the area.

We open Chapter 2, called 'Reading Advertising', with a vignette of how advertising can be experienced phenomenologically in order to open the question of how audiences encounter and understand advertising as an intimate part of our lived experience of on- and offline media. Central to the production and the consumption of advertising today is the smartphone, amongst other Wi-Fi-enabled devices, and we say a little about how this device has changed the experience of advertising for half the world's population. The chapter goes on to locate the approach of the book in a tradition of literary and interpretive works of scholarship that showed advertising to be something not merely processed as information, but read and interpreted, as text. Chapter 3, 'Understanding Advertisements as Social Texts', continues the literary analogy applied to advertising and dovetails this with more detail on Genette's theory of the paratext, noting how Genette's work has been adapted from its original deployment in paper-based literature to extend to texts of electronic media. The chapter offers many examples of advertisements that deploy subtle (and not-so-subtle) literary techniques. Chapter 4, 'Paratexts and the Meaning of the Brand', turns to an examination of the idea of branding, without which it is hard to understand the point of advertising. Advertising and branding are treated as separate disciplines, but this separation is artificial – the practical logic of either can only be understood with reference to the other. The chapter looks back at the origins of commercial branding before bringing us up do date with case examples of iconic brands, in order to explore the role brands play as nexuses of cultural meaning. Our examples illustrate the ambiguous character of consumer brands[24] as communicative phenomena and demonstrate some of the ways in which advertising paratexts operate to inscribe meanings into the ambiguous or empty space of the brand. This idea, of course, challenges the conventional brand management notions that brands have essential qualities that should not be violated by advertisers and are expressed in brand strategy documents as the inviolable brand 'values', 'personality' or brand 'essence'. We don't argue that brands are mere vapour: they have material substance, visual identity, history, and their values can be important too, to a point, if they have some. We simply argue that the apparent qualities of brands are only there by virtue of the paratexts that surround them, and, further, that these qualities are far from essential. Paratextual theory can underpin a shift from the reification of brand values in what Douglas Holt calls the 'mindshare' approach to brand management,[25] to open up an approach to understanding the brand as a repository of cultural meaning.

At this point in the book we feel that we should address an old question of how advertisements 'work', and this is the main subject of Chapter 5. For both academic and practical purposes it is important to consider the motives of the people who make advertising. Too many academic studies ignore the complex and enigmatic ways in which advertisements are created, while too many managerial how-to books fail to provide any theoretical explanation of why their claims should be believed. We ask the question 'How Does Advertising "Work"?' with 'work' within quotation marks because of the simplistic assumptions implied in this metaphor when applied to advertising; these being, that it is one thing, that it does one thing, and that what it does can be addressed in a common-sense way through a common-sense question. We try to treat this point in an uncomplicated way in order to connect the idea of advertising as a text with the popular understanding of advertising as a device that brands use to sell stuff.

We feel that it is necessary to do this in order to move to the next step of the book which addresses storytelling in advertisements, in Chapter 6: 'Storytelling and Paratextual Advertising'. In this chapter we focus on brands as sources of, and as projections of, consumer stories. The idea of storytelling has become very popular in brand consulting and advertising. It seems intuitive that brands and ads tell stories, broadly conceived, but equally, most brand communications do not tell a fully developed story, as such. Rather, advertising (at least, creative advertising) acts as a suggestive yet open text that fires the audience's imagination and cues stories that can be projected into, or otherwise connected with, the brand. We discuss some of the practitioner and academic efforts at articulating brand storytelling methods, poetic effects and systems, but we also show how the very notion of storytelling becomes distorted when it is applied to brands that create communications that often have little in the way of a plot, a protagonist or a narrative, and do not follow the traditional story arc of conflict through to resolution. Paratexts, of course, are not exactly storytelling vehicles, they are routes of entry into stories that signal how the stories should be read. We try to illustrate how this distinction shapes the understanding of advertising as brand storytelling.

The traditional source of most creative advertising, the ad agency, is facing increasing challenges from changing client priorities, competition from media agencies, in-house operations and brand consultancies, not to mention from the massive continuing disruption provided by the global digital platforms and the changing media consumption patterns of consumers. In fact, the creative ad agency system is in an existential crisis and traditional certainties about account team roles and creative advertising development processes are rapidly breaking down. In Chapter 7, 'Paratextual Advertising Strategy', we examine some of the implications of our perspective for the ways in which advertising is made, and what purposes it might serve. We resort to the business book cliché of the acronymic tick-box, how-to, heuristic framework for paratextual branding and advertising strategy. We do not claim that the model is a recipe for success, but we use it to try to summarise the major practical implications of our perspective for doing advertising strategy. In Chapter 8, 'Paratextual Advertising and the Future', we summarise the key issues of conceiving of advertisements as brand paratexts as we see them, with an eye to the future of research in the area.

THE COLLAPSE OF OLD ADVERTISING CATEGORIES

The examples of promotional media content, or as we call it all, advertising, that we mention in this book, are all a bit different from each other, but they share some important features. For one thing, the promotional motive is implicit in most of them – there is nothing sales oriented about the content. Rather, they are conceived as forms of information or entertainment for people to use, enjoy and share on social media. They are, in effect, great publicity for the brands they feature, and publicity happens also to be great advertising.[26] Or, to put it another way, they are advertisements that are made to look like information or entertainment. The primary purpose for which audiences engage with these examples of media content is not to obtain information about offers from brand owners – it is to be entertained or diverted. Such content might also pop up in a digital search for a brand, adding entertainment value to the other attributes of the brand.

Many scholars and practitioners of marketing would be quick to explain why the examples we have listed differ from advertising, and from each other, tactically, and in execution. This wouldn't be wrong – indeed, many of these advertising genre categories have their own universes of specialised professional associations and qualifications, textbooks, skill sets and career paths, even though a brand client would often expect a large advertising agency to be knowledgeable in all of them in order to construct a campaign containing any combination of these elements.[27] In this book we draw on the ideas of Genette on paratextuality, and the extensions of his ideas by media, film and TV scholars, to explain why we think it is useful to conceive of such diverse forms of promotional media content as having a distinct commonality that can be understood through paratextual theory. We maintain that this paratextual level of commonality is analytically important because it offers a route into a deeper understanding of how advertising operates within a convergent[28] media environment. We also maintain that it is connects with current trends in advertising and branding practice, both operationally and strategically, as many agencies now operate multi-disciplinary teams reflecting the broadened media and creative horizons for advertising. The boundaries separating the old sub-categories of marketing communications and the promotional mix are becoming increasingly blurred[29] as digital platforms throw up new, hybrid forms of advertising communication that cut across the boundaries. We think it is important to consider the sweep of advertising as a superordinate category of communication within and around all media content, not only because this perspective provides a more coherent basis for brand communication strategy, but also because that is the spirit in which it is now consumed.

We use the term advertising to cover all media content that has, at some level, a promotional motive, from social media content to street billboards, TV spots to radio ads, branded packaging to branded content, product placement to sponsored influencer posts, not excluding the content produced by social media users such as likes, shares and reviews of, or comments on, brands, products and consumer experiences. This is a broader definition of advertising than is common in introductory advertising and marketing (or 'marketing communications') textbooks. Advertising is often defined as a paid-for promotional message on a mass medium with an identifiable source, but our view is that this definition has never been adequate to cover the vast realm of promotional media content in which the promotional motive is implicit, the author/source uncertain, and/or the payment indirect or absent. What is more, the area to which the traditional definition does apply is rapidly shrinking as a proportion of global adspend, as a result of the changes in the media infrastructure. A narrow definition of advertising or of the other elements of the old 'promotional mix' or 'communications mix' is useful for media planners pricing a campaign to demarcate between, say, search advertising, OOH executions, influencer content, paid social, online reviews and a viral video, but what interests us analytically is what unifies these various techniques rather than what separates them.

Today, for the increasing numbers around the world who use digitally enabled devices for most of their media consumption,[30] brands are ubiquitous features in an almost seamless experience of news, information and entertainment, often accessible on one, Wi-Fi-enabled device. Much of this branded media content is not overtly promotional but is in effect publicity, and much of it is not paid for in the sense that it is hosted or shared, and, often, created, at no cost to the brand. Clearly, from a managerial perspective, there are important tactical differences between promotional texts (as we acknowledge above) and we do not seek to minimise these differences. We hope to demonstrate in the book that understanding how media paratexts can inflect the meaning of brands can contribute not only to a more coherent and unified theoretical understanding of contemporary advertising, but also to a stronger analytical purview on how advertising, broadly conceived, inflects the meaning of the brands featured within it. We want to show that the idea of paratexts captures something of the connectedness of all promotional media content in an era characterised by the deep integration of the digital with the non-digital experience – a post-digital era. We also want to show that, by thinking of promotional media content as a series of paratexts, we are able to reframe ideas about what advertising can do for brands, and how it does it. Finally, we hope to contribute to a broader conversation about how brands, and media paratexts in general, come to mean things in the world.

THE DECLINE OF THE BIG CREATIVE IDEA IN ADVERTISING

Our perspective on creative advertising is not an attempt to revive old saws and ignore the complexity of the new digital advertising environment. We do, though, want to try to retain the best of the old ways while adapting them to the new realities. We will say more about how advertising was once made, and how this needs to change, as the book progresses, but for now it is worth emphasising one obvious difference between advertising in the 1960s and 1970s, and today. Imagine the classic 1960s advertising campaign based on a Big Creative Idea, say, in the UK, the Cadbury's Smash Martians and The Lady Loves Milk Tray, Nestle's Here Comes the Milky Bar Kid, heavyweight Henry Cooper 'Splashing It All Over', the Oxo Family, or in the USA, Coke's I'd Like to Teach the World to Sing or, later, 'Meet Joe Greene', Wendy's 'Where's the Beef'? or the irritatingly mnemonic Budweiser 'Whassup?' ads.[31] The Big Idea would often be 'owned' by a star creative and executed through a 20-second TV commercial that might be aired several times a day for six months before a variation on the theme was produced. There would be no doubt that the commercial was paid for by, and intended solely to promote, one brand. The ad would become part of everyday conversation[32] such was the audience reach and impact of the latest big campaign in a time when real-time TV viewing audiences in the Western world were several times greater than today.[33] Perhaps, for a time, the popular meaning of a brand might be defined by reference to a particular ad, as if the ad served as a mediated version of a primary text, that is, a primary source of meaning, about the brand.

Today, TV retains a unique impact as an advertising medium, but it lies amongst a fully integrated constellation of digitally enabled platforms across which brands pass the consumer view in a kinetic frenzy. Rarely do we see Big Ideas leading an ad campaign, and on the occasions that we do, the Big Idea is 'spreadable', which means it is executed in many iterations across multiple platforms to fit within the consumers' crowded media landscape. Brands today rarely provide the prime-time talking point of an evening's TV viewing. Rather, they wheedle their way into our deeply divided attention through a haze of other media content.

Advertising can be seen as a mere footnote in profound changes in technology, communication, media, consumption and society. Technology has unquestionably driven changes in media consumption and production that have heavily influenced not only how, what and when we buy, but that also shift the demarcation line between production and consumption. As prosumers[34] we have presided over the disintermediation of supply chains. Consumers now take on a lot of the virtual work of building and sustaining brands through seeking out, reviewing, discussing, sharing and even distributing[35] brands, goods and services. Even so, advertising is by no means merely the froth on the heady brew of digital capitalism. Advertising has emerged as the primary business model of the new digital platforms and the logic of advertising is driving significant waves of changes in media and consumption. In turn, the digital platforms have distilled advertising into a unified promotion, order reconciliation, service and purchase experience with a few clicks of the cursor. Advertising is now part of a technologically converged retail system.

Since the emergence of consumer culture, advertising has held a contradictory place as a form of communication;[36] it is both reviled and lionised, ignored and over-analysed, dismissed as a trivial sideshow to the real stuff of business and society, and blamed for every manner of social ill because of its role in perpetuating and amplifying damaging cultural norms of over-consumption, negative stereotypes of race, gender and body type, individualism and so on. Advertising has always occupied this precarious social space.[37] In its contemporary manifestations it is no less worthy of examination.

We will use the literary concept of the paratext to explore how consumers, advertising and brands interact with, and influence the meaning of, each other. In so doing we hope to make two main contributions. Firstly, we hope to contribute a new perspective to the long and vibrant tradition of research in marketing,[38] advertising and consumer studies[39] that has adapted literary theorisations but that, to date, has almost entirely neglected the idea of the paratext. We acknowledge that the idea of the paratext is well established in academic media, film and television studies research, and it has been used to analyse marketing and advertising in non-business academic fields, particularly film and media studies of movie and TV show promotion. We will draw on examples of this broad range of work to help open a route into the idea of paratextual advertising and branding from our marketing/business perspective. If it seems surprising to the casual reader that an idea that is commonplace in one academic discipline has been ignored in another, obviously connected, discipline, it was surprising to us, too. As far as we know, our piece in the journal *Marketing Theory*[40] was the first in our discipline that explicitly applied paratextual theory to a focused analysis of advertising. Our second objective, connected to the first, is to open up a new practical understanding of how promotional communication operates in the digital era. To this end, we will apply the ideas in the book to many practical examples in the hope that the book will prove of interest not only to scholars and students, but also to marketing and advertising professionals, and indeed to anyone who has an interest in the way that marketing, advertising and media affect our lives.

NEW, HYBRID ADVERTISING GENRES

We refer above to the implicit presence of brands in content. This implies an action by the reader that links the content to the brand by drawing on their wider socio-cultural knowledge. If we watch a sports event on TV that ends with an interview with the winner as he or she wears their sponsor's logo, we complete the gestalt, if we have become acculturated to the sponsor's logo. Paratextual content can sometimes cue a silent intertext – the connection between the brand and the content does not have to be made explicit because the reader (the consumer who is exposed to the content) has some prior understanding that helps them make this connection. The use of silent intertexts has become a common feature of advertising where, for example, a MacDonald's arch, or a Nike Swoosh is artfully placed into some content in the knowledge that most of the target audience will recognise the promotional intent. The silent intertext is the more powerfully suggestive for being implicit, partly because the viewer is actively complicit in construing the meaning. Silent intertexts might also operate where it becomes known amongst the in-group that a piece of media content, like, say, the YouTube video of a New York café paranormal event mentioned earlier was, in fact, staged by a movie studio to promote the remake of the movie *Carrie*.[41] In some content such as this, and other examples such as the Dove virals, the branding was absent or subtle in initial executions in order to stimulate conversations and curiosity about the source and motive. Consumers, especially young consumers, enjoy the game of spotting the ways in which brands try to manipulate them[42] and brands know that enigmatic brand communications soon generate a buzz of social media talk, especially if some in the audience have found out the truth and have a story to tell. Everyone enjoys being the owner of proprietary knowledge. In paratextual branding, subtlety often pays because many consumers arettarcted to polysemous forms of advertising that do not have a clearly evident message than they are to messaging that beats them over the head with a sales message.

It is important to state that, although there are new, hybrid forms of advertising communication being enabled by digital media, paratextuality is not just about the form, it is also about the content. Indeed, if one posits the brand as a notional primary text, conventional advertising can also be seen to operate as paratext, confusing the issue further. Earlier, we suggested that the modern advertising environment is characterised by increased velocity of circulation of brand content. Another characteristic is the decreased cultural authority of terrestrial TV and print media in relation to digital media (and of marketing in general[43]). TV and print had a vividly enhanced cultural standing in the media landscape before digital media subsumed them into its vast plains. The iconic TV and print ads of the 1950s–1990s were treated as if they were primary texts, by audiences, and by academic analysts. A single print or TV ad could attain such a standing that it lent itself to a deconstructive treatment as a source from which cultural meaning emanated (we outline some of this pioneering research later). We suggest that the paratextual character of such content, less apparent in a pre-digital media environment, is heightened in a digital environment because of the velocity and volume of circulating brand content, along with the reduction in cultural authority of TV and print and concomitant changes in patterns and habits of media consumption.

As we touched upon earlier, our paratextual approach chimes with the shift in the logic of promotion, from the explicit, to the implicit, from hard sell, to soft sell, and from sales, to brand building.[44] The hard-sell ad remains, of course, especially in programmatic social media advertising with its 'call to action' designed to wrest the casual browsers' grip from the edge of the digital sales funnel so they topple into its very bowels and become the 0–5% who not only click on the ad, but also buy the advertised brand.[45] Social media hard-sell ads notwithstanding, the marriage of entertainment and advertising has meant that audiences frequently encounter brands as a passive presence in video, film and TV, video games and advergames and so on, while a lot of print and TV advertising is designed to look a lot like entertainment.

One example of the way ostensibly traditional ads often look like entertainment is the UK TV spots for the Nationwide Bank 'Voices' campaign that consisted of non-famous people reading out their poems about daily life direct to camera.[46] The TV ads (made by VCCP, the same agency that created the ubiquitous comparethemarket.com meerkats mentioned above) are accompanied by a YouTube channel to which anyone can upload their own poems.[47] Like all good ad campaigns, it is underpinned by a strategy – the idea that the bank cares about the same things as ordinary people. To the more literal minded client, this kind of oblique message seems wilfully obscure, hence the perpetual tension between agencies and client around how much trust can be placed in the audience's interpretive ability. Once again, this is not new – in the 1960s Bill Bernbach famously pushed trust in the audience far beyond what most in the industry thought possible at the time with his radical use of ironic self-deprecation in VW's Beetle campaigns.[48] Some in the industry maintain that the best advertising should indeed be entertaining and fun for its own sake, as well as saying something about the brand (such as Paul Feldwick[49]), because fame is what brands need, and famous ads make the brands they advertise famous too.

Strangely, there has always been tension in the ad industry between the idea that ads should be fun and entertaining, and the idea that they should, instead, be informative and sales oriented – advertising creativity has often been seen as a 'problem' to be controlled rather than the industry's foremost asset.[50] We discuss this tension later in the book. Our point here, though, is that ads that are intrinsically entertaining[51] illustrate well the paratextual character of advertising in the sense that they rarely make explicit declarations about the brand – their role in the meaning of the brand is secondary. Rather, like the iconic 1985 Levi's 501 jeans ad, Laundrette,[52] they invest the brand with fame, along with a raft of implicit associations, and sales follow. The perceived risk of such 'hero' ads from financially stretched clients is that they are enjoyed by many people who will never have any interest in buying what is advertised, but it is wrong to infer from this that the non-selling exposure is a 'waste' of resource or a case of inefficient ad targeting (and few clients are more financially stressed than Levi's were at that time – Laundrette was a last throw of the dice, with the brand's future placed in the hands of BBH, and specifically Barbara Nokes[53] and Paul Hegarty). The fame simply ensures that the brand is memorable, and liked, for a huge audience reach, and that is usually enough to move the sales mountain. Laundrette tapped into a faint cultural memory of denim-wearing 1950s movie heroes such as James Dean and Marlon Brando and amplified an American myth of youth, sex appeal, rebellious freedom and denim jeans. A decade later, the cultural meaning of jeans had shifted again, American provenance was no longer so marketable, the myth had been forgotten, and lots of very un-cool middle-aged people were wearing 501s. Huge audiences had experienced Laundrette as a threshold into an American myth that had denim jeans at its very centre. Even an iconic ad such as this could not be understood as a primary text – it was a completed work, as such, and worthy of analysis no doubt, but its relation to the brand, and its engagement with the audience, was paratextual.

CONCLUDING COMMENTS

In Chapter 1 we have outlined the main ideas of the book. We have drawn on many examples of creative advertisements to illustrate what we see are the key features of paraxtextual advertising, and to show why we think there is a need for a new way of understanding advertising as a totality of brand communication, as it is evolving under today's pressing technological, industrial and cultural influences. In Chapter 2 we will look a little more closely at the idea of an advertisement as something that is read and interpreted as a text by an audience, drawing on some of the pioneering research literature that introduced literary forms of analysis into business, management and related fields of scholarship.

NOTES

1. Paul Grainge, Moments and opportunities: Interstitials and the promotional imagination of BBC iPlayer. *Critical Studies in Television*, 12(2) (2017) 139–155. DOI: 10.1177/1749602017698158.
2. Gérard Genette, *Paratexts: Thresholds of Interpretation*, trans. Jane E. Lewin (1997), University of Cambridge Press.
3. See Constantine V. Nakassis, Brand, citationality, performativity. *American Anthropologist*, 114(4) (2012) 624–638. DOI: 10.1111/j.1548-1433.2012.0 1511.x.
4. For elaborations on convergence see Henry Jenkins, *Convergence Culture: Where Old and New Media Collide* (2006), New York University Press.
5. Anthony Patterson, Yusra Khogeer and Julia Hodgson, How to create an influential anthropomorphic mascot: Literary musings on marketing, make-believe, and meerkats. *Journal of Marketing Management*, 29(1–2) (2013) 69–85. DOI: 10.1080/0267257x.2012.759992.
6. Dove: You're More Beautiful Than You Think. https://www.youtube.com/watch?v=litXW91UauE
7. Volvo: Epic Split. https://www.youtube.com/watch?v=M7FIvfx5J10
8. BMW The Hire: Ambush. https://www.youtube.com/watch?v= GW11Lez4elc
9. Lazar Dzamic and Justin Kirby, *The Definitive Guide to Strategic Content Marketing: Perspectives, Issues, Challenges and Solutions* (2019), Kogan Page.
10. Not such a far-fetched notion in the early 1900s – France at this time was the world's foremost car manufacturer.
11. https://www.comparethemarket.com/meerkat/meet-the-meerkats/
12. https://www.aldi.co.uk/kevin
13. Stephen Brown and Sharon Ponsonby-McCabe, They're gr-r-reat! Introduction to the special issue. *Journal of Marketing Management*, 29(1–2) (2013) 1–4. DOI: 10.1080/0267257X.2012.762184.

14. The term influencer marketing is common, but in most sponsored influencer content what is being done is not marketing, but advertising.
15. A piece about product placement in literature by the first author in online publication *The Conversation*. https://theconversation.com/literatures-long -love-affair-with-product-placement-34384
16. Chris Hackley and Rungpaka Amy Hackley née Tiwsakul, Observations: Unpaid product placement. *International Journal of Advertising*, 31(4) (2012) 703–718. DOI: 10.2501/IJA-31-4-703-718. Although branded content and product placement are well-developed commercial techniques, most brands on TV are still there simply because the TV show set designer needed a scene prop for that morning's shoot. So many thousands of hours of TV programming are made every year that there simply isn't the time to arrange contracts for every item needed in a scene, and the assumption is that most brands would have no objection to a TV appearance, especially if the brand is sourced from a prop supplier with whom the brand has a contract.
17. For more on this see Chris Hackley and Rungpaka Amy Hackley, *Advertising and Promotion*, 5th Edition (2021), Sage.
18. Industry estimates vary, but we are assuming that of the circa US$600bn annual global expenditure on advertising of all kinds, roughly half is cate-gorised as 'digital', which includes all advertising content on digital media, and the rest, mostly made up of traditional media advertising, i.e. TV, print, OOH (Out Of Home), radio, cinema. One excellent source of ad industry info is The Drum, which published its annual adspend projections for 2022 here: https://www.thedrum.com/news/2021/07/12/digital-power-104 -recovery-global-ad-spend
19. The term content marketing is more commonly used, but we feel that most of the practices under this heading are more accurately described as advertising.
20. There are many examples of video content in which the branding and the true source and motive is initially very subtle or absent, designed to tease the curiosity of audiences, before the true nature of the content is slowly made public, e.g. the 2013 *Carrie* stunt to promote the remake of the movie: https://www.youtube.com/watch?v=VlOxlSOr3_M
21. There is no attempt to deceive in examples like the Dove virals, but the branding is sometimes subtle, at least when the video is first released, in contrast to, say, fake restaurant or product reviews.
22. For an outstanding example, see Jonathan Gray, *Show Sold Separately: Promos, Spoilers, and Other Media Paratexts* (2010), New York University Press.
23. A useful introduction is Gérard Genette and Marie Maclean, Introduction to the paratext. *New Literary History*, 22(2) (1991) 261–272. DOI: 10.2307/469037. Genette's works on his theory of transtextuality were orig-inally published in French some years before being translated for English publication, this example having been translated by Marie Maclean.
24. Stephen Brown, Pierre McDonagh and Clifford J. Shultz, II, *Titanic*: Consuming the myths and meanings of an ambiguous brand. *Journal of Consumer Research*, 40(4) (2013) 595–614. DOI: 10.1086/671474.

25. We discuss Holt and branding more in Chapter 4: the mindshare approach is Holt's description of Al Riess and Jack Trout's well-known ideas on brand positioning, and, specifically, the idea that a brand is a cognitive phenomenon in that it subsists as a bundle of subjective perceptions in the mind of the consumer.
26. There is an ongoing debate in advertising research about how advertising 'works', which we pick up in Chapter 5. For now it may be useful to state that one school of how ads work insists that the object of an ad is to persuade the viewer to buy the advertised thing, in the 'advertising is salesmanship in print' tradition made famous by John E. Kennedy. The other school insists that advertisements seldom persuade anyone in the way that a salesperson might but, rather, act as longer-term publicity, increasing the social and psychological space the brand occupies, and increasing sales and market share as a consequence of the publicity effect (see Andrew Ehrenberg, Neil Barnard, Rachel Kennedy and Helen Bloom, Brand advertising as creative publicity. *Journal of Advertising Research*, 42(4) (2002) 7–18. DOI: 10.2501/JAR-42-4-7-18. The first author outlines the various theories of advertising effects in Chris Hackley, Theorizing advertising: Managerial, scientific and cultural approaches, chapter 6 in Pauline MacLaran, Michael Saren, Barbara Stern and Mark Tadajewski (Eds) *The Sage Handbook of Marketing Theory* (2010), Sage, pp. 89–107. A lot of the key papers referred to in that piece are available in Chris Hackley (Ed.) *Advertising* (2009), Sage.
27. Advertising, brand or media agencies which have the main responsibility for a client's campaign will often buy in specialist expertise if it isn't available in-house.
28. Henry Jenkins, *Convergence Culture: Where Old and New Media Collide* (2006), New York University Press.
29. Chris Hackley, Advertising, marketing and PR: Deepening mutuality amidst a convergent media landscape, chapter 4 in Jonathan Hardy, Iain MacRury and Helen Powell (Eds) *The Advertising Handbook (Media Practice)*, 3rd Edn (2018), Routledge, pp. 58–73.
30. https://www.pwc.com/gx/en/news-room/press-releases/2019/consumers -moving-away-from-traditional-forms-of-entertainment-and-media -consumption.html
31. These ads are all easily searchable on video sharing sites such as YouTube.
32. Stephanie O'Donohoe, Advertising uses and gratifications. *European Journal of Marketing*, 28(8/9) (1994) 52–75. DOI: 10.1108/03090569410145706.
33. In the UK, up to half the entire population would sometimes watch the most popular TV shows, and the ads.
34. George Ritzer and Nathan Jurgenson, Production, consumption, prosumption: The nature of capitalism in the age of the digital 'prosumer'. *Journal of Consumer Culture*, 10(1) (2010) 13–36. 1469-5405 DOI: 10.1177/1469540509354673.
35. Almost anyone can establish themselves as an intermediary on selling platforms such as eBay.
36. See Guy Cook, *The Discourse of Advertising* (2001), Routledge.

37. William Leiss, Stephen Kline, Sut Jhally, Jackie Botterill and Kyle Asquith, *Social Communication in Advertising: Consumption in the Mediated Marketplace* (2018), Routledge.
38. Stephen Brown, Marketing and literature: The anxiety of academic influence. *Journal of Marketing*, 63(1) (1999) 1–15. Accessed 16 May 2021. DOI: 10.2307/1251997.
39. Barbara B. Stern, Literary criticism and consumer research: Overview and illustrative analysis. *Journal of Consumer Research*, 16(3) (1989) 322–334. Accessed 16 May 2021. http://www.jstor.org/stable/2489513
40. Chris Hackley and Rungpaka Amy Hackley, Advertising at the threshold: Paratextual promotion in the era of media convergence. *Marketing Theory*, 19(2) (2019) 195–215. DOI: 10.1177/1470593118787581.
41. https://www.youtube.com/watch?v=4ir5q6foPCM
42. Rungpaka Amy Tiwsakul and Chris Hackley, The meanings of 'Kod-sa-na-faeng' – Young adults' experiences of television product placement in the UK and Thailand, in Ann L. McGill and Sharon Shavitt (Eds) *Advances in Consumer Research*, 36th Edn (2009), Association for Consumer Research. https://www.acrwebsite.org/volumes/v36/naacr_vol36_52.pdf
43. Douglas Holt refers to the declining cultural authority of marketing in: Why do brands cause trouble? A dialectical theory of consumer culture and branding. *Journal of Consumer Research*, 29(1) (2002) 70–90. Accessed 16 May 2021. DOI: 10.1086/339922.
44. For one account of this phenomenon see Chris Hackley, Advertising, marketing and PR: Deepening mutuality amidst a convergent media landscape, chapter 4 in Jonathan Hardy, Iain MacRury and Helen Powell (Eds) *The Advertising Handbook (Media Practice)*, 3rd Edn (2018) Routledge, pp. 58–73.
45. We discuss digital advertising in more detail later, for now here is an account of the sales funnel and the infamous click-through rate (CTR) metric: https://www.omniconvert.com/blog/uses-click-rate-measuring-funnel-conversion-rate/. While this is a more recent piece with calculations of CTRs and 'Conversion' or sales rates by David Chaffey, Ecommerce conversion rates 20/21 – How do yours compare? *Smart Insights* (2021): https://www.smartinsights.com/ecommerce/ecommerce-analytics/ecommerce-conversion-rates/
46. https://www.thedrum.com/creative-works/project/vccp-nationwide-voices
47. https://www.youtube.com/playlist?list=PLP8zX0EDIZJvHIkahbhp_ELYbBjyqw5F1
48. For an account of Bernbach's work on VW and its implications for the ad industry, see https://medium.com/theagency/the-ad-that-changed-advertising-18291a67488c
49. Paul Feldwick, *Why Does the Pedlar Sing? What Creativity Really Means in Advertising* (2021), Matador.
50. See Chris Hackley and Arthur J. Kover, The trouble with creatives: Negotiating creative identity in advertising agencies. *International Journal of Advertising*, 26(1) (2007) 63–78. DOI: 10.1080/02650487.2007.11072996.

51. There is a nice compendium of many of the most famous TV ads from the past 50 years, put together by Thinkbox: https://www.thinkbox.tv/creative/3 -great-ads-i-had-nothing-to-do-with/the-most-inspiring-ads-ever/
52. See the ad here: https://www.youtube.com/watch?v=Q56M5OZS1A8
53. https://www.independent.co.uk/news/media/cv-barbara-nokes-creative -director-grey-1287575.html

2. Reading advertising

INTRODUCTION

In Chapter 1 we outlined the idea that advertisements, which we define very broadly as media content that includes brands in some way or other, can be understood as having a distinctively paratextual character, drawing on and adapting Gérard Genette's literary concept of the paratext. We suggested that, although this is so of advertisements in all ages, the literary analogy is especially suited to the convergence era of low-attention, short-form, high-volume and high-velocity advertising consumed across multiple digital platforms. We acknowledge that low attention and high velocity are not new in advertising. What we suggest is that the environment in which we consume media has changed, and the ways in which we engage with advertising media in that environment have changed, and paratextual theory can help us to understand how these changes are playing out. We see Genette's key idea, that the paratext acts as a threshold through which the primary text is entered, as central to understanding the relationship between the kind of implicit advertising that is now common, and brands. Just as a work of literary (or any other) art is given meaning by the paratexts that surround it, so too are brands given meaning by the advertising paratexts that surround them.

In Chapter 2, we open with a vignette of the lived experience of advertising, as we imagine it, in order to set out a context for the way advertising is often experienced today. We then go back over some of the key business school research literature that introduced literary and other disciplines of interpretive theory into the agenda for advertising research, in order to locate our perspective as a development of this broad trajectory of advertising theory.

THE LIVED EXPERIENCE OF ADVERTISING

Central to the matter of which we write is, of course, the smartphone. Daniel Miller and colleagues,[1] in their 2021 global ethnographic study of smartphone use, use the analogy of the smartphone as transportal home, and while somewhat counterintuitive, the analogy resonates more, the more you think about it. Home is, after all, the place where we feel comfortable, and where we spend most of our time. It is a location for personal interactions with our closest family and friends. It is where we store our most precious memories such as family photo albums, music and movie collections, holiday snaps: it is the place where we express our unguarded opinions, and it is a place that is uniquely individualised to reflect our character and personality. The phone, and the home, are where we find solace, where we relax, read the newspaper, watch TV, listen to the radio. The smartphone can fulfil all of these functions, in a digitally extended form, at least for those in the world who own them (which is around half of the world's population, and rising[2]).

There are negative aspects of having so much invested in the smartphone too – both home and phone are where not only our own networks and loved ones can always reach us, but also where bad actors know where we are. We can be spied upon, we can receive unwanted and aggressive communications, and we can be burgled, or hacked, spammed or phished. We can be subjected to huge volumes of junk advertising or aggressive sales calls. The smartphone is also a device that blurs the demarcation between home and work, to the extent that for millions of people post-COVID-19 there is no longer any distinction – we are always at work, just as we are always at home, when we have our smartphone. The smartphone compels our attention like a mesmeric personal TV, encyclopaedia and work assistant combined, and it has become normalised to drop out of any social context to lose oneself for a time in smartphone absorption. We live within the smartphone, in the sense that we can become psychologically absent, momentarily, even when in physical proximity with others.

Needless to say, advertisers are very much aware of the value of the smartphone as an advertising billboard that we carry with us 24/7 and consult around 58 times per day, adding up to an average of more than three hours per day looking at a smartphone screen,[3] according to some estimates (and potentially far more – research from the USA poses a figure of 12 hours per day per adult interacting with media on all devices).[4] The problem for advertisers is not so much that we spend so much time on the smartphone, but that we spend some time not looking at it. The smartphone is essentially an advertising medium, or at least most of the applications we run on smartphones are funded by an advertising business model. But we use the smartphone within an offline environment with which we cannot avoid interacting. Advertising operates in an era in which digital media operate intimately and continually within the offline world. We flip back and forth between the online and offline worlds multiple times a day. This is certainly new since the smartphone first appeared in the 1990s[5] and our dependence on it has risen. The offline and online, or digital and analogue, are becoming more closely entwined, to the extent that there are experiments with microchips implanted into willing humans to do away with the need to carry a receiver. But before we stray from our topic into a discussion on the Wi-Fi-enabled, digitally enhanced human, we ask you to consider an everyday scenario in which advertising is encountered.

Imagine it's a Monday morning and you are standing on a rail station platform, waiting for a delayed train to work. As you walked from the barrier to your usual waiting spot on the platform you took in a six-sheet poster ad, shop signage, and a huge 96-sheet[6] billboard, noticing none of the ads has been changed since Friday. A rainstorm is just waning, and the smooth concrete platform has an attractive watery sheen. You escape the remaining spatters of raindrops by squeezing into the crowd under the edge of the overhead canopy that extends from the station building. Under the shelter of the canopy, you take your phone from your coat pocket and tap on the Facebook icon. It gives you a lovely family photograph of a day out by the sea taken and posted on this day eight years ago. You share it, forgetting that your settings allow anyone to view the picture, not just your family, then you scroll through posts on your news feed. You realise that there are more sponsored posts and 'marketplace' ads for second-hand goods than there are organic posts. You swipe up the screen to close the Facebook app and open the BBC News app for the headlines, then look at your Garmin app to see how much deep sleep you had last night. Hmm, just 35 minutes again. No wonder you're tired. You check your Amex credit card statement. You tap on the Instagram app and scroll down, realising that every fourth post is a sponsored one. A goods train screams by and the crowd recoils from the powerful slipstream, huddling further under the canopy for safety. But it is the morning commute in London, and nobody is rude enough to make excessive physical contact with other people. You return to your phone and have a skim of the Mail Online app for a fix of prurience or outrage, and then you remember you were going to buy a book. You tap on the Amazon app, search for the book, read some reviews, buy the book so it'll be delivered to your home by the morning. You have a sense that someone is looking at you, and your eyes rise to meet the adoring gaze of a young person with cheekbones that might have been designed by Dali ... in a glossy full page Gucci magazine ad the person in front of you is reading. You look down in case you're thought rude for reading over someone's shoulder.

Just then, your attention is diverted by the urgent ping of a sound notification. Several people around you hear it and check their phones – you are the lucky one, it was your phone. You are indeed a part of the active world, with friends, connections, commitments. Smugly, you open the text, only to read a message from a slightly boring friend telling you about a second-hand car they just bought from an online service called Cinch. You hope that your fellow platform-dwellers might think the ping was your PA telling you that a government minister is urgently requesting a meeting. You respond to the text, you've seen the TV ads for the brand, fronted by a reality TV show star with unfeasibly white teeth who now seems to get lots of TV presenting gigs, and you write to your friend that the car looks lovely. It doesn't. You check the train arrivals board. Still delayed. You go to YouTube, click on a movie trailer, watch an ad. The opening scene of the trailer is set in a Starbucks, and the actor is wearing an Omega watch.

As you stand on the station platform your peripheral vision and hearing gather still more stimuli even while you're browsing your phone. Distracted by the brakes screeching on another train, you look up and notice litter by the track. In just a few milliseconds you register the familiar colour schemes and brand names of a McDonald's Happy Meal box, a Subway sandwich wrapper, a dented Tennant's lager can. You become briefly aware of snippets of barely audible conversations, tannoy announcements of arrivals, departures and delays, you recognise a melody from someone's headphones. You notice the wafting smell of sausage rolls that you know comes from a Greggs bakery because you walked past it a moment ago. You notice a brand logo on the handbag of a lady in front, then you notice some more branding, on a train coach. You return to the movie trailer after checking the arrivals board. Still delayed. The actor in the trailer is driving away in a Mercedes, his Starbucks coffee cup in the drinks holder.

Suffice to say, you[7] are registering dozens of brands in the course of this kinaesthetic scanning process. Brands are both in front, and in the background. They're just, there, like the ether. None of them is the point, they are just, well, thresholds, into other worlds. Your awareness of them doesn't feel reluctant, there's no impulse to resist their hectoring – they're not invading your consciousness, they're not screaming at you.

They're passive, they're just saying 'hi!' You don't think about them, or even notice most of them consciously, but you register them all, at least the familiar ones, and most of them are familiar. Some people have gone to a lot of trouble and expense to reach you with these images of branding. Is there a point to it all? Is there some subtle and sinister science at work in the way these brands are segued into your lived experience? Or are you being treated as a shrimping net? Throw enough offers at you and maybe one will stick in the net?

The urban phenomenon of feeling as if you're braced against a blizzard of advertising is not new, even if some of the technology is. In the 1800s, *Punch* magazine[8] satirised the cacophony of advertising on the teeming streets of Victorian London as shop signage and window displays, logo-bedecked vehicles, walls full of advertising posters and notices, 'sandwich' board men with their wearable advertisements ('sandwich boards') and street hawkers all competed for the momentary attention of passers-by. For some 200 years, advertising has been waving desperately at us, trying to get us to notice it, look at it, listen to it, read it, think and talk about it. Today, we are not so far from the scenes in the 2002 Tom Cruise movie *Minority Report*,[9] with face recognition, chatbots and other AI applications enhancing advertising technology.

On occasion, an advertisement can create huge impact with millions of people. Even the fading emperor of advertising, the TV spot, can still do the business if there is a real-time audience to see it. For example, Superbowl ads[10] in the USA or, in the UK, the annual Christmas retail ads,[11] are dwelt upon by viewers, viewed again and again for enjoyment, iterated in other forms, discussed by business press and media commentators, analysed by academics, and reproduced in case study compilations and scholarly works. More typically, though, the presence of brands and branding has become a taken-for-granted part of our everyday experience. Like our commuter above, advertising doesn't so much come at us like hailstones – rather, it is simply part of our phenomenological experience of life.

THE INCOMPLETENESS OF THE MEDIA PARATEXT

Ads have always had to break through consumers' divided attention, and they have always been paratextual in character. What is new is the velocity and speed with which these curiously incomplete texts circulate and are consumed. Their incompleteness might be a feature of their form, their content, or of the way that we engage with them. They are fragmented texts that we must place a context around in order to ascribe meaning to them. To an alien visiting earth for the first time, they would have no meaning. They have meaning for us through the meaning we invest into them, drawing on our cultural priming. Brand paratexts activate our imaginations through their very incompleteness. They are fragmented indices, and we can repair the indexicality of each symbol, logo, colour combination or brand name that we see, with astonishing speed and fluency, so thorough has been our immersive socialisation in a brand-world. A mere fragment of discarded wrapper bearing a torn corner of a logo is enough to simultaneously invoke the brand name, the visual identity, the concept, memories of the store design, product range, the times you consumed the product. We learn a rich vocabulary of branding as brand paratexts are mirrored and multiplied through our experience of on- and offline media.

For all the fashionable talk of brand 'storytelling' (which we fashionably talk about in Chapter 6), not to mention compelling creative executions, 'engaging' the consumer and super-clever algorithms that know what you're thinking when you're browsing social media, what can you read into an ad that you view for ten-thousandths of a second as you scroll through your social media news feed, or that you glance at as you wait for a train? Well, quite a lot as it happens. We hardly read these texts as we would a book or article, but we know that we can read, or at least recognise and register, short words and symbols with astonishing speed. It can take as little as ten-thousandths of a second to recognise a single letter[12] but research suggests that we can process all the letters in a word simultaneously for the purpose of word recognition, meaning that a word that is presented in a large, distinctive font, as most brand names are, could be recognised in not much longer than that. Our commuter is not paying focused attention to the ads, but then focused attention is not necessarily required for brands, words and meanings to be registered. A lot of business research into advertising still makes the assumption that focused attention of the audience is a precondition for an ad registering on consciousness, but Robert Heath and Paul Feldwick[13] among others have shown that focused attention is not necessarily a prerequisite for advertising to have some effect. For example, where one can hear the jingle or dialogue from a TV when one is in a different room getting a drink, there can be a sense of recognition of the brand.[14] This is one of the reasons for the effectiveness of radio advertising, where the radio plays in the background of a workplace, car or household, audible but not the subject of focused attention. At some level, most of the time, we do register sensory information that is in the periphery of our consciousness, including advertising images and sounds. This is encouraging news for advertisers who spend millions on digital display advertising, since some practitioner studies have suggested that as few as 3% of these ads are noticed at all on some platforms, and, where they are noticed, the average dwell time (time spent looking at the ad) is about one second.[15] This does represent a challenge to advertisers who would benefit from elevating audience attention into engagement, but our point here is that attention in itself is not necessarily the commodity that advertisers need to be buying – they also benefit from acquiring space in the audiences' lived experience.

The meaning-making process, then, the way we read meaning into these incomplete texts, is not done to us – it is done by us. These texts without a context, these indexicals, are given context by our need to complete the gestalt. The incompleteness of the text opens up the brand as an ambiguous space[16] into which we might project all manner of meanings, cued by the brand's paratexts. In many advertising textbooks, the transmission model of mass communication is used to illustrate how the one thing advertising must never do, is to craft a message that might be misunderstood by the receiver. Paratextual theory shows us that, in fact, ambiguity is a key virtue in branding and advertising (as Stefano Puntoni and colleagues point out in their work on strategic advertising polysemy[17]). Advertising paratexts do not need to have a message in the sense of a declarative, explicit statement. They only need to appear as part of the texture of our lives.

The attention we pay to advertisements of all kinds, then, is, on the face of it, more divided, dispersed and fleeting than it typically might have been 40 years ago, and the ads are more fragmented and discontinuous, yet they also hold a more intimate presence in our lives. As we negotiate between the demands on our online and offline experience we see ads juxtaposed with our most intimate moments, our family photographs, our social media posts, comments and shares with friends and family. Ads are everywhere that we engage with media, which is, everywhere. Not only are ads, and brands, everywhere, they are everywhere all the time. Our mobile phones are packed with apps – each of which is a powerful advertisement and an inducement to tap – that we see every time we look at the phone. It is hardly necessary to say that this 'post-digital' media environment for advertising in which off- and online media form a seam-less part of consumer experience is qualitatively different to the environment consumers faced in earlier times. But does this really change how we should understand advertising? To try to place some research context around this question we will outline a small selection of the literary and related work on advertising that has established the field in business and management.

ADVERTISING AND BUSINESS RESEARCH

We will outline below how literary and other interpretive theories of advertising began to intrude into university business school research in the 1980s. The shift in focus that literary perspectives on advertising meant for business school researchers is alluded to in a 1995 paper by Mark Ritson[18] and Richard Elliott,[19] in which they state: 'The prevailing paradigm which has dominated the study of advertising for over forty years has been that of the information-centred or information processing model of consumer behaviour' (p. 113, citing Grant McCracken[20] amongst others). The idea of advertisements as texts that can be read, rather than data to be processed, introduced an element of interpretation that sat uneasily with the business school ideology of scientific management techniques and scientific research methods.

Ritson and Elliott pointed out that the assumption that advertising furnishes consumers with information with which said consumers then make rational buying decisions is flawed in that it oversimplifies the ways in which consumers engage with advertising, and it also ignores the role of meaning in social communication. They and like-minded researchers recognised that advertising is understood in a complex context that requires cultural knowledge in order to understand the meanings implied in the ad. In other words, consumers are not machines processing advertisements as sensory data input. Rather, consumers are interpreting creatures who have to acquire a form of cultural literacy in order to successfully read advertisements, as we would to understand any other practice or discourse in the world. Data input has to be organised by means of learned cultural understanding. We learn to read advertisements pragmatically, that is, to acquire an understanding of their meaning and motive.

While the notion of advertising literacy is by no means new, we claim that understanding advertising as paratextual communication adds a previously neglected element to the literary perspective on advertising, at least in our field of business and management. Our argument for the novelty of paratextual theory in advertising is not that the application of our take on Genette's work to advertising and other media content is new per se, but that the research literature on advertising in the business and management areas has neglected to theorise advertising's paratextual character, while research from media, TV and film studies has not extended the idea of paratextual promotion beyond media brands to consider its application to the full range of brands and content of every sector. We use Genette's ideas selectively and understand them in the light of poststructuralist theories of reader response and intertextuality.

Interpretive theory presents a challenge for a discipline in which theory has often been of the back-of-the-napkin variety; that is, mnemonic systems that have no empirical support but seem to be superficially applicable as heuristic devices for managers. For napkin-theory in marketing see, for example, the Marketing Mix (the Four Ps), numerous varieties of marketing strategy, product lifecycle and company growth matrices, and the ubiquitous Attention-Interest-Desire-Action[21] framework of advertising effectiveness. As Ritson and Elliott point out, where it is grounded in systematically generated and analysed data sets, advertising theory has had a tendency to be constructed around experimental methods, typically based on participants who individually view one advertisement at a time in a viewing booth.[22] The objection to this used to be that it lacked ecological validity since TV ads, at least, were usually viewed while watching TV in a household and therefore the reception of an ad should be understood as a social rather than a purely cognitive phenomenon. We should nuance that view today given the capacity of mobile media devices to draw us into a curiously solipsistic and solitary interaction with the smartphone that is, at the same time, inherently social.

As Daniel Miller and colleagues point out in the study we refer to above, we can be in a social setting and our phone periodically draws us into a solipsistic world – we can be alone, focusing on a media image, amongst a crowd of friends. A recent (2021) viral video showed a groom's delight at the sight of his bride, but while she was en route towards him to be joined in matrimony, he reached into his pocket, took out his phone and stared at the screen,[23] apparently finding his message notification more compelling than what ought to be one of the defining moments of his life. This does not mean that the years of wasted research using viewing booths has suddenly become ecologically valid – advertising is no less of a social phenomenon for being viewed alone. It simply means that the inherent sociality of advertising has taken on a different, digitally mediated, character.

So, in the brief outline of research that follows, we will, more or less, ignore the experimental and survey research that dominates the business and management field[24] to look at a small selection of literature that represents a rough lineage of literary research on advertising/branding within our business and management field.[25]

BARBARA STERN AND THE LITERARY SCHOOL OF ADVERTISING RESEARCH

Barbara Stern[26] is credited with introducing literary theory into consumer and marketing research,[27] arguing that consumers do not simply 'process' advertising as data input but read and actively interpret advertisements as if they were texts. Stern advocated literary research as part of a humanities-led agenda in advertising and consumer research[28] that emphasised the interpretive character of human understanding. The idea of cultural phenomena as texts was then, and remains, common across the social sciences and humanities, though at the time it was rarely acknowledged in business and management research. A social text is sometimes described as anything that can be described, hence most social, cultural and psychological[29] phenomena are reducible to text. The import of this for advertising research is significant. It means advertising audiences are not data processing machines but readers – the idea of the text permits them some latitude in the ways they interpret marketing communication. The locus of meaning shifts from the makers of the ad to the audience who read it. Stern's contributions paved the way for more broadly interpretive perspectives on advertising research from poststructuralist traditions in anthropology and qualitative sociology.

The idea that advertising and other marketing communications can be understood as data inputs intended to programme the desired attitudinal processing in target consumers took a hold on the field of business research at the turn of the century and retains that hold today, in spite of critiques such as those of Ritson and Elliott (mentioned above). This is not just about a principled ontological difference in business research between the realists and the social constructivists. It was also a deeply political issue when Stern published. Since the Ford and Carnegie reports of the 1950s[30] university business school research has legitimised itself as a social scientific university subject by adopting a natural science model. The research agenda is shaped by the available methods. To this day, although there is much inter-disciplinary work, there remains a sensitivity over the role of the humanities in business research. If it can't be expressed in numbers, is it really rigorous enough to count as science? Barbara Stern entered that fray with aplomb and opened up new possibilities for research in the field that drew not on cognitive science and information processing theory, but on the humanities. The idea of advertisements as social texts was by no means new in the greater scheme of things. For example, Judith Williamson[31] analysed not what ads mean, but how they mean, using semiotics to show how advertisements could be vehicles for ideology. But business and management research in general often takes several years before someone realises that an idea that is well established in another discipline could actually be pretty useful.[32] Stern drew on Wolfgang Iser's[33] reader-response theory to show that the meaning of a text resides in the space between text and reader. In her critique of the use of the Shannon–Weaver transmission model of communication[34] for advertising research Stern[35] pointed out that there are important differences between spoken and mediated communication, and between human and machine communication, that are ignored by many of the old but still popular models of advertising communication.[36] Chris Miles subsequently developed Stern's work into a dialogic model of advertising communication.[37]

Stern's ideas caught on, and many other researchers followed with ideas from literary theory, linguistics and other areas of interpretive theory drawn upon to analyse many advertising styles, types and genres. For example, Linda Scott applied an interpretive approach to analyse the rhetoric of advertising jingles,[38] and later used reader-response theory in her studies of the consumer response to advertising.[39] In the abstract to the piece on advertising jingles, Scott powerfully expresses a limitation of the cognitive and experimental research thus:

> Studies of music in advertising have tended to characterize music as a nonsemantic, affective stimulus working independently of meaning or context. This implicit theory is reflected in methodology and procedures that separate music from its syntax of verbal and visual elements. Consequently, the consumer's ability to judge and interpret music as part of an overall rhetorical intention is overlooked. (P. 223)

Treating music as 'language-like' suggests that consumers have the power and volition to listen, as we would read text, and interpret the meaning of music in advertisements.

Anecdotally, it is well known in the advertising business that music tracks in advertisements make people 'turn their heads' to pay attention if they recognise the music. Music has the power to evoke memories for consumers who might identify a piece of music with a life stage or life event, hence the meaning of the music, and by implication the way it inflects the meaning of the brand, can be deeply personal. For the brand, the point is that iconic music has this power for many people: millions share cultural reference points even if the precise way they relate to these reference points is deeply personal. Millions of people might recall a particular piece of popular music as a cultural reference point in their lives, even though each of them connects the music to memories of a different life, different events and locations, and a different group of friends (for more on advertising, music and personal identity see Giana Eckhardt and Alan Bradshaw's work in *Marketing Theory*[40]). Music brings a meaningfulness to the advertisement and the brand that is both personal and collective, it supplies an evocative emotional resonance that can be nuanced to fit intimately into many lives. Later in the book we say more about this with reference to Scott's 2018 book with Alan Bradshaw, about the advertising campaign that established sportswear brand Nike as a force in popular culture: *Advertising Revolution*.

THEORISING THE IMPLICIT IN ADVERTISEMENTS

Much of the literary work we refer to in this chapter is attempting to theorise what is implicit in advertisements, that is, what is not expressly stated in the advertisement but which, nonetheless, may be construed by the reader. Implicit communication is very important for advertising. It means that advertisers can get around the problem of taboo topics or regulations forbidding certain claims, by implying them instead. So, for example, if ads claimed explicitly that brand x makes the user more sexually attractive, socially successful or happier, it would be dismissed as an absurd, improper and unjustifiable claim. However, ads are able to juxtapose the brand with implicit values and associations which are no less powerful or obvious for being implicit, but which are far less likely to invoke the derision of consumers or the ire of regulators. Implicit communication is arguably the richest and most important element of advertising, yet it lies outwith the scope of the most popular cognitive and information processing-based, business school theories of advertising.

The meanings readers draw from advertisements may be subjective, but they are not arbitrary. People who share a cultural milieu also share a common vocabulary of cultural sign systems. These sign systems are artfully tapped into by creative advertisers[41] to make ads that resonate for the reader. To put this another way, advertisers use the vocabulary of popular culture to make texts that open up spaces of meaning. This is seen, for example, in a study by Edward McQuarrie and David Glen Mick who combined methodological perspectives to achieve a nuanced analysis of consumer responses to the visual rhetoric of advertisements,[42] building on Mick's earlier work on semiotics.[43] While Mick's influences were anthropological, we can see an overlap between the use of semiotics to analyse visual elements of advertising, and the origins of semiotics (or semiology) in linguistics.[44]

Returning to literary analyses of advertising, Stephen Brown and colleagues used the work of Russian literary critic Mikhail Bakhtin to frame a gendered reading of a single advertisement.[45] This paper, typically of work in this tradition, implicitly treats the advertisement as a finished work and a primary source of meaning. The analysed ad seems, on the face of it, to be treated as if it were a primary text. Stephanie O'Donohoe's work challenged the conventional idea in mainstream business school research that the consumer is a passive receiver and processor of the advertising message by showing that advertising does not only do things to people, but people do things with advertising.[46] That is, people use advertising creatively in their daily lives as a discourse informing their own vernacular communication, an observation also made by Mark Ritson and Richard Elliott in their ethnographic study of the way adolescents use talk about advertisements to negotiate their social lives.[47] In Ritson and Elliott's work, school students would talk about the latest ad with their friends (Ritson enterprisingly took a job as a teaching assistant and listened to the out-of-class chatting) and the authors showed that the ads the students found funny or striking played a role in negotiating group membership and their sense of social identity. In these, as in the other works we cite, there is no sense of the paratextual character of the ad – it seems to be treated as a primary source of meanings that are not accepted hegemonically but interpreted by readers. What is common in these approaches is that the meanings of the ad are not located solely within the text of the ad. Rather, they are open, to a degree, to the interpretation of the reader, and this in turn depends on the cultural context in which the ad is read.

O'Donohoe drew attention to the importance of the work of Julia Kristeva[48] to advertising research with Kristeva's work on the role of intertextuality in advertising.[49] Kristeva's idea that text assumes meaning through its connection to, and existence within, a network of other texts is also the point of departure for Genette's ideas on paratextuality. According to theories of intertextuality, advertisements are not self-contained units of meaning. Rather, they subsist within

a complex web of mutually referential intertexts. Interpreting advertisements requires that readers draw upon their skills of media and cultural
literacy.[50] Many ads refer intertextually to other ads, to movies, to news
events, to popular trends or fashions: all rely for their meaning in some
way or degree on the reader grasping the intertextual references to other
social texts. The intertextual reference might be explicit, but, more typically, intertextual references are implicit. For example, in the UK a series
of video ads for the Aldi supermarket chain featured the Kevin the Carrot
character in scenes that parodied well-known Christmas stories, movies
and other Christmas ads.[51] In order to understand these ads, the reader
would require knowledge of the other movies, stories and ads, along with
an understanding that advertisements sometimes engage in intertextual
parody of other media.

PERSPECTIVES FROM PRAGMATICS AND LINGUISTICS

Outside business schools, researchers from other disciplines have
turned their attention to advertising. We have already mentioned Judith
Williamson's well-known semiotic/ideological account of advertisements. Structuralist semiotics falls short in its account of advertising
meaning, though, in that it fails to account fully for the variability of
interpretation of given signs.

For example, Keiko Tanaka[52] focused on the pragmatics of advertising language to highlight the distinction between what is explicit in
advertising communication (what Tanaka calls 'ostensive') and what is
implicit (Tanaka's label for this is 'covert'). It is an oft-repeated truism
that up to 90% of the meaning of human face-to-face communication is
communicated implicitly, relying on readings of body language, gesture,
appearance, vocal intonation and minute shifts of facial expression, so
it is surprising that, even today, the implicit in advertisements receives
such little attention from mainstream business school research. Implicit
communication in advertisements can entail all manner of linguistic and
non-linguistic tropes and techniques, including colour schemes, visual
background scenes, body juxtapositions, the gestures, tone and manner
of actors, the musical background, and many other elements of the
advertising *mise en scène*.[53] Work on linguistic rhetoric points out that
what is left unsaid can be more communicatively powerfully than what is
explicitly stated. What is implicit is to some degree subjective, although
socially mediated, and depends on the interpretive frame of the reader.

Studies that approach advertising from a reader perspective can articulate the meanings that are read into particular advertisements by particular readers, as do David Glen Mick and Claus Buhl in their 1992 paper on meaning in advertising,[54] and these readings might deviate completely from explicit messages that the ad designers might have intended to encode into the ad. There are many examples of failures of encoding in advertising creative strategy, from the classic 1959 Strand cigarettes TV ad[55] that was hugely popular but didn't sell cigarettes, to the 2017 Kendall Jenner Pepsi ad[56] that was withdrawn a few days after launch because of the derision with which it was received.

Applied linguist Guy Cook[57] studied advertising as a form of discourse and concluded that advertising fulfils a human need for communicative play. Cook's work draws attention to (amongst many other things) the context effects of advertising interpretation – we will read an advertisement differently depending on the other texts within which it is situated. A print ad in *The Sun* newspaper, one in *Tatler* magazine, a digital billboard in Times Square, New York, a TV ad in the interval of a daily lunchtime soap opera, or one during a break in the US Superbowl coverage, all are subject to differing inflections of meaning from the context in which they are seen and read. TV advertising, in particular, confers a frisson of prestige on to the brand by virtue of the medium. Even a cheaply produced TV ad aired off-peak on a minor channel is occupying the same technological space as ads for global brands with multi-million dollar budgets and Hollywood production values, implying that the brand that has a presence on TV has a certain status, and certain resources, and is at the least aspiring to be a player in the brand scene. In the digital era TV has somehow retained some of its prestige as a major platform in spite of the general collapse of real-time viewing figures.

The idea inherent in the transmission model of advertising communication that an advertisement must have a clear and unambiguous sales message is confounded by the many ads (since Bill Bernbach introduced irony into advertising[58] in the 1960s) that make use of polysemic visual or narrative executions which are enigmatic, confusing, open to various interpretations and, yet, compelling, at least for those in the target group who 'get' the ad and buy into the strategic polysemy (see the earlier comment in this chapter on Stefano Puntoni and colleagues' work on advertising polysemy). Ads that intrigue, tease and even confound, draw the viewer into the game of interpretation, deepening 'engagement'. Sometimes they do so to create a sense that the target audience is a rather exclusive in-group, the members of which get the joke, as for example in a long-running series of copy-driven ads for the *Economist* magazine by David Abbott of Abbott Mead Vickers. Print and OOH (Out Of Home) ads with copy like "'I never read the Economist" – management trainee, aged 42', 'Lose the ability to slip out of meetings unnoticed' and 'Insider reading', all presented in the distinctive font and colours of the magazine, speak to the intelligence of the target readership because while the out-group is still pondering the meaning of the ad, 'Enocomsit rdeeras avhe lradaye wrkode ti out'.[59] Abbott began the now famous *Economist* campaign back in 1984, showing that with regard to implicit communication at least, advertising practitioners have been well ahead of most business school researchers for a very long time.

CONCLUDING COMMENTS

In Chapter 2 we wanted to set this book in a broader context of interpretive theorisations of advertising from literary and other humanities' perspectives. We have referred to a number of older studies in order to establish the trajectory of these traditions in business school research journals. In Chapter 6 we will bring this up to date with some recent published studies of advertising which use a literary theoretical standpoint. The small and selective outline of these trajectories we offer in Chapter 2 illustrates some of the ways in which interpretive theory, including concepts and ideas from literary studies, linguistics, semiotics and anthropology, has been brought to bear on questions around how advertising becomes meaningful in the act of being read by its audience. Many of these studies, though, drew on assumptions from formalist literary criticism about close reading forms of textual analysis. That is, they assumed that a given advertisement could be conceived for the purposes of analysis as a primary text, and that the meaning of that text is contained within the text. They challenged many of the taken-for-granted assumptions of experimental and survey research about advertising's main purpose and its effects, but they also assumed that, in some way, the advertisement as text held a primary status.

Having looked at the idea of the consumer as a reader of advertisements, in Chapter 3 we need to look a little more deeply at the idea of advertisements as texts. In particular, we need to address the idea of the social text that extends beyond the work itself.

NOTES

1. Daniel Miller, Laila Abed Rabho, Patrick Awondo, Maya de Vries, Marilia Duque, Pauline Garvey, Laura Haapio-Kirk, Charlotte Hawkins, Alfonso Otaegui, Shireen Walton and Xinyuan Wang, *The Global Smartphone Beyond a Youth Technology* (2021), UCL Press. https:// discovery.ucl.ac.uk/id/eprint/10126930/1/The-Global-Smartphone.pdf ?fbclid=IwAR3ayaTSgZvCWfqqsYN3Ytz5WQWfKXMX49DKjW_ 5mR4IzWc1jZLEaQODXZw

2. It is estimated that about half of the world's population owns smartphones, but around 70% of people own mobile devices, projected to rise to 90% by 2023. https://www.bankmycell.com/blog/how-many-phones-are-in-the -world

3. https://elitecontentmarketer.com/screen-time-statistics/

4. Nielsen, *Nielsen Total Audience Report* (2020), February.

5. https://www.textrequest.com/blog/history-evolution-smartphone/

6. https://www.billboardadvertising.org.uk/outdoor/train/greater-manchester/ marylebone/

7. Please adapt this male POV for your desired gender.

8. For example, this one from circa 1890: https://punch.photoshelter.com/image ?&_bqG=0&_bqH=eJzzNzHPN8xPKc8MrjIK9zELj8xNj7fM9fYrLjCxM jS0MjQwAGEg6RnvEuxsm5hSllpUklmcmZeuBhaJd_RzsS0BskODXYPi PV1sQ0Gqs7yyMk2DkvJyPNPV4h2dQ2xLi4uCUxOLkjPU3EGK3E GKkqvcU3xd_RPDIiLVnEGiAPkkK2Q-&GI_ID=

9. https://www.youtube.com/watch?v=7bXJ_obaiYQ

10. Being talked about is the key to the most successful advertising, as Professor Cristel Russell points out in this 2021 piece about the value of Superbowl ads: https://www.psychologytoday.com/us/blog/the-savvy-consumer/202102/the -power-superbowl-ads-social-audience

11. Here is one of the many web articles that show the Christmas retail ads: https://www.housebeautiful.com/uk/christmas-adverts-round-up/

12. See G. Sperling, A model for visual memory tasks. *Human Factors*, 5 (1963) 19–31.

13. Robert Heath and Paul Feldwick, Fifty years using the wrong model of advertising. *International Journal of Market Research*, 50(1) (2008) 29–59.

14. We will not digress here into the hoax of subliminal advertising, which is quite another thing, but we do touch on it briefly later in the book.

15. For example, see this 2016 study on audience attention in digital display advertising by Lumen: https://s3.eu-west-2.amazonaws.com/lumenresearch -website-static/White+Paper+2017+Bassett%2C+D+Value+of+Media+ Environment.pdf

16. See, for example, Stephen Brown, *Brands and Branding* (2016), Sage.

17. Stefano Puntoni, Jonathan Schroeder and Mark Ritson, Meaning matters. *Journal of Advertising*, 39(2) (2010) 51–64. DOI: 10.2753/ JOA0091-3367390204.

18. This was in another life for Ritson, who these days no longer focuses on academic research papers, and instead works as an excellent columnist:

https://www.marketingweek.com/mark-ritson/, and is one of the world's top Marketing gurus: https://mba.marketingweek.com/?creative=530965127645 &keyword=mark%20ritson&matchtype=e&network=g&device=c&gclid =EAIaIQobChMIueCforOw8gIVEuJ3Ch1OeAYjEAAYASAAEgLlpfD _BwE

19. Mark Ritson and Richard Elliott, Advertising literacy and the social signification of cultural meaning, in Flemming Hansen (Ed.) *European Advances in Consumer Research Volume 2* (1995), Association for Consumer Research, pp. 113–117. Available at: https://www.acrwebsite.org/volumes/ 11084/volumes/e02/E-02

20. Grant McCracken, Advertising: Meaning or information, in Melanie Wallendorf and Paul Anderson (Eds) *Advances in Consumer Research Volume 14* (1987), Association for Consumer Research, pp. 121–124. Available at: https://www.acrwebsite.org/volumes/6667/volumes/v14/na-14

21. A-I-D-A was not quite a back-of-the-napkin theory, but it was principally about the psychology of personal selling, adapted and popularised by Edward K. Strong in *The Psychology of Selling and Advertising* in 1925. Connected to this is John E. Kennedy's famous and much-repeated assertion that advertising is 'salesmanship in print' (for more on Kennedy, see https:// www.scientificadvertising.com/authors/jek/).

22. Mark Ritson and Richard Elliott's article, The social uses of advertising: An ethnographic study of adolescent advertising audiences. *Journal of Consumer Research*, 26(3) (1999) 260–277. DOI: 10.1086/209562. This contains a critique of the viewing booth tendency in advertising research.

23. https://metro.co.uk/2021/06/10/man-checks-phone-as-bride-walks-down -the-aisle-and-people-call-for-divorce-14747674/

24. For an account of the three main schools of research in advertising, see Chris Hackley, Theorizing advertising: Managerial, scientific and cultural approaches, chapter 6 in Pauline MacLaran, Michael Saren, Barbara Stern and Mark Tadajewski (Eds) *The Sage Handbook of Marketing Theory* (2010), Sage, pp. 89–107.

25. We apologise for the cumbersome scope-setting subject lists we resort to in the book. By way of explanation, the sociology and politics of academia has it that academics working in one area are encouraged (or often compelled) to publish their research in journals that are within specified fields or sub-fields. Indeed, career progression, or just keeping one's job, often depends upon doing so. These disciplinary silos are often dominated by paradigmatic assumptions about the most robust or legitimate research methods. It all gets quite complicated – for example, advertising courses are often taught in communications departments in universities in the USA, and more usually in university business schools in the UK, while consumer research is (bizarrely) often treated as if it is a different discipline to marketing, and, equally bizarre, media, TV and film studies research is often ignored in business school marketing departments. There is, admittedly, quite a lot of cross- and inter-disciplinary overlap, and this book is obviously an example, but these divisions dominate the structure and political

demarcations of subjects in university business school departments, hence our clunky disciplinary scope-setting.

26. Barbara B. Stern, Literary criticism and consumer research: Overview and illustrative analysis. *Journal of Consumer Research*, 16(3) (1989) 322–334. DOI: 10.1086/209218.
27. See also Stephen Brown, Bow to stern: Can literary theory plumb an unfathomable brand? *Marketing Theory*, 15(4) (2016) 445–464. DOI: 10.1177/1470593115572670.
28. See also, for example, Barbera B. Stern and Jonathan E. Schroeder, Interpretive methodology from art and literary criticism: A humanistic approach to advertising imagery. *European Journal of Marketing*, 28(8–9) (1994) 114–132. DOI: 10.1108/03090569410067659.
29. Jonathan Potter, Peter Stringer and Margaret Wetherell, *Social Texts and Context: Literature and Social Psychology* (1984), Routledge and Kegan Paul.
30. Discussed in Frank C. Pierson, *The Education of American Businessmen* (1959), McGraw Hill.
31. Judith Williamson, *The Semiotics of Advertising* (1978), Sage.
32. And here we are.
33. Wolfgang Iser, The reading process: A phenomenological approach. *New Literary History*, 3(2) (1972) 279–299.
34. An outline of the Shannon–Weaver transmission model of communication can be found here: https://www.communicationtheory.org/shannon-and -weaver-model-of-communication/
35. Barbara B. Stern, A revised communication model for advertising: Multiple dimensions of the source, the message, and the recipient. *Journal of Advertising*, 23(2) (1994) 5–15. DOI: 10.1080/00913367.1994.10673438.
36. Discussed in Chris Hackley, Theorizing advertising: Managerial, scientific and cultural approaches, chapter 6 in Pauline MacLaran, Michael Saren, Barbara Stern and Mark Tadajewski (Eds) *The Sage Handbook of Marketing Theory* (2010), Sage, pp. 89–107.
37. Chris Miles, A cybernetic communication model for advertising. *Marketing Theory*, 7(4) (2007) 307–334.
38. Linda M. Scott, Understanding jingles and needle drop: A rhetorical approach to music in advertising. *Journal of Consumer Research*, 17(2) (1990) 223–236. DOI: 10.1086/208552.
39. Linda M. Scott, The bridge from text to mind: Adapting reader-response theory for consumer research. *Journal of Consumer Research*, 21(3) (1994) 461–490. DOI: 10.1086/209411.
40. Giana M. Eckhardt and Alan Bradshaw, The erasure of antagonisms between popular music and advertising. *Marketing Theory*, 14(2) (2014) 167–183. DOI: 10.1177/1470593114521452.
41. The cultural intermediaries: Anne M. Cronin, Regimes of mediation: Advertising practitioners as cultural intermediaries? *Consumption Markets & Culture*, 7(4) (2004) 349–369. DOI: 10.1080/1025386042000316315.

42. Edward F. McQuarrie and David Glen Mick, Visual rhetoric in advertising: Text-interpretive, experimental, and reader-response analyses. *Journal of Consumer Research*, 26(1) (1999) 37–54. DOI: 10.1086/209549.

43. David Glen Mick, Consumer research and semiotics: Exploring the morphology of signs, symbols and significance. *Journal of Consumer Research*, 13(2) (1986) 196–213. DOI: 10.1086/209060.

44. Especially in the Ferdinand de Saussure tradition of semiology (the study of linguistic signs), although in the broader tradition of semiotics (the study of any signs whatsoever) Charles Sanders Peirce has become more common in the deconstruction of advertising signs and symbols. For introductions see Francesco Bellini (Ed.) *Charles S. Peirce. Selected Writings on Semiotics, 1894–1912* (Semiotics, Communication and Cognition) (2020), Du Gruyter Mouton; and Ferdinand de Saussure, *Course in General Linguistics* (2013 reprint edition), Bloomsbury Academic.

45. Stephen Brown, Lorna Stevens and Pauline Maclaran, I can't believe it's not Bakhtin!: Literary theory, postmodern advertising, and the gender agenda. *Journal of Advertising,* 28(1) (1999) 11–24. DOI: 10.1080/00913367.1999.10673573.

46. Stephnie O'Donohoe, Advertising uses and gratifications. *European Journal of Marketing*, 28(8/9) (1994) 52–75. DOI: 10.1108/03090569410145706.

47. Mark Ritson and Richard Elliott, The social uses of advertising: An ethnographic study of adolescent advertising audiences. *Journal of Consumer Research*, 26(3) (1999) 260–277. DOI: 10.1086/209562.

48. Julia Kristeva, *Desire in Language: A Semiotic Approach to Literature and Art* (1980), Columbia University Press.

49. Stephanie O'Donohoe, Raiding the postmodern pantry: Advertising intertextuality and the young adult audience. *European Journal of Marketing*, 3(34) (1997) 234–253. DOI: 10.1108/03090569710162344.

50. We think it is possible to argue that digitally enabled consumers might enjoy an advanced media literacy in the sense of being able to identify and connect many images and symbols of advertising and consumer culture. The question of whether this advanced media literacy includes a truly critical understanding of the motives, interests and persuasive methods behind digital communications would be much more difficult to argue for, and we don't make that claim, since we believe that *critical* media literacy skills seem to be sadly deficient, evidenced by the rise of flat-earther, QAnon and other groundless conspiracy theories that circulate on social media.

51. Some examples of the Kevin the Carrot Aldi ads can be found here: https://www.youtube.com/watch?v=HXSM0b1H1WE

52. Keiko Tanaka, *Advertising Language: A Pragmatic Approach to Advertisements in Britain and Japan* (1994), Routledge.

53. The film theory concept of *mise en scène* and its application in product placement advertising is discussed in Chris Hackley, *Marketing in Context: Setting the Scene* (2013), Palgrave MacMmillan. See: http://www.palgraveconnect.com/pc/doifinder/10.1057/9781137297112

54. David Glen Mick and Claus Buhl, A meaning-based model of advertis-
    ing experiences. *Journal of Consumer Research*, 19(3) (1992), 317–338.
    JSTOR: www.jstor.org/stable/2489392
55. 1959, Strand Cigarettes TV spot – the theme tune became a huge chart hit,
    and the actor became a star, but the ad strategy, encapsulated in the strapline
    'You're never alone with a Strand', failed to resonate with smokers who saw
    their vice not as a solitary activity but a social one. https://www.youtube
    .com/watch?v=WjBHUQEiTPw
56. The Kendall Jenner Pepsi ad tried to play on the Black Lives Matter protests,
    but was interpreted as trivialising them. https://www.youtube.com/watch?v
    =uwvAgDCOdU4
57. Guy Cook, *The Discourse of Advertising* (2001), Routledge.
58. Bill Bernbach was an American ad man who became legendary in the trans-
    atlantic advertising world in the 1960s for redefining what was understood
    about creativity in advertising. There are many accounts of the man and
    his work on the internet, this is one of them: https://medium.com/swlh/bill
    -bernbach-on-creativity-6fbebce57b2b
59. For more examples, see: https://www.honeycopy.com/copywritingblog/
    economist-ads

3. Understanding advertisements as social texts

INTRODUCTION

In Chapter 3 we want to revisit the idea of understanding advertisements as texts. We will also look a little more closely at some of Gérard Genette's ideas, as set out in his work *Paratexts: Thresholds of Interpretation* (1997).[1] We want to consider the matter not just of what advertising texts mean, but how do they mean, and how are they read? The idea of the social text is so commonplace in the humanities and social sciences that it might seem laboured to return to it, but we do so for two main reasons. One is that the notion might seem counterintuitive to those familiar only with the information processing approach to advertising, which, as we've said, dominates the assumptions of much business school research and managerial literature. The scientific legitimacy of university business school research has been heavily invested in 'hard' science, i.e. quantitative methods and realist ontological assumptions, since Frank Pierson's influential but misunderstood 1959 book on the university education of American businesspeople.[2] Useful though it may be to understand the physiological and cognitive responses to advertisements, it is equally important to understand how audiences make sense of these data inputs, and we feel that the idea of advertisements as texts and audiences as readers does so.

The other main reason we revisit the idea of the text is that we want to examine in more detail some of the assumptions of the textual metaphor in the light of Genette's ideas, since there are clearly different ways of reading different texts. For example, a reader would not engage with footnotes or a preface in quite the same way as they would the chapters of a novel, just as a media audience would not usually engage with a classified ad, a radio ad, a social media display ad, or a 20-second TV ad, in quite the same way. We want to try to tease out some of the nuances of the idea of reading when applied to media texts, and we will pick up some of these issues in Chapter 6 when we will look at how ideas about storytelling might, or might not, apply to advertising texts and paratexts.

ADS, TEXTS, AND MEANING

In Chapter 2 we touched on Wolfgang Iser's notion that the meaning of a literary work such as a novel is not delimited by the author's intention but, rather, resides in the space between text and reader. As Iser described: '... the literary work cannot be completely identical with the text ... the text only takes on life when it is realised ... the convergence of text and reader brings the literary work into existence'.[3] A novel has thousands of words for the author to make their intention as clear as possible, yet, for Iser, there still remain innumerable gaps of meaning in the text that will be filled in different ways by different readers. An advertisement, in contrast, is a highly condensed and constrained form of text. How much more open to interpretation, then, must this form of social text be than a novel?

It is true that an advertisement that simply exhorts the reader to buy brand x has a far simpler narrative structure than a novel, but most ads try to be less direct and more enigmatic than this in order to capture the interest of readers. It is, in fact, quite difficult to imagine that even the crudest form of advertisement does not require some order of culturally mediated interpretation. The slogan 'Buy X!' for example, juxtaposed with a visual image of the brand, is a declarative exhortation that makes little sense as a printed instruction – why does the author imagine that they have the authority to command obedience? And to whom is the exhortation aimed? A reader socialised into the practices of advertising texts would understand that the ad is not an order but, in fact, is a plea, directed at the reader.

The idea of text allows us to identify some of the less explicit persuasive elements of advertisements. It is not unusual to see business and management textbooks asserting that persuasive advertising was invented in the 1960s, as if advertisers before then had the copyrighting nous of neanderthals. As media technology and Western economies developed in the 1950s, we did indeed see many vivid examples of lifestyle and status advertising that deployed striking new aesthetic styles enabled by new media technology. But even before TV, glossy magazines and radio, advertisers were no slouches in the arts of motivation. For example, Catherine Harbour's archival analysis of London newspapers from the late 17th and early 18th centuries demonstrates that classified ads for music concerts exploited class, status and the sense of self and social identity as part of their persuasive repertoire, with copy aimed at 'persons of quality'.[4] The authors of the ads understood that a musical concert was far more than a musical concert, but a networking and publicity opportunity that reflected aspirations of social status and identity.

This was just part of the subtle and persuasive marketing that existed at the time and was exemplified in the pottery, arms and medicines industries as well as music.[5] Eighteenth-century entrepreneurs like Thomas Holloway[6] (whose profits established a building later to become a college of the University of London[7]) and, before Holloway, Josiah Wedgewood,[8] the pottery pioneer, and his contemporary, gun magnate Samuel Colt,[9] not to mention circus impresario Phineas Taylor Barnum,[10] were all astute marketers and advertisers who lacked nothing in their intuitive skills of consumer insight and artful copywriting. They seemed to understand that advertising was a form of paratextual publicity that could invest the brand with qualities that reflected the deep aspirations and fantasies of the audience.

We adopt the idea of text as a sweeping analytical unit that embraces all genres and forms not only of literary texts (the poem, the novel, the screenplay, the libretto and so forth) but, in its wider accepted usage in social science and humanities' scholarship, anything that can be described. Social texts are comprised of words and language, but also of other forms of symbolic communication, such as images. When we talk about advertisements as social texts, we are talking not only about the copy or script of an advertisement, but also the imagery, logos and any other signs and symbols entailed in the text. The metaphor of the text reflects a poststructuralist movement in social science since the 1970s (Jacques Derrida's work being a notable landmark[11]) that rejected the idea that signs and symbols have a fixed and immutable underlying meaning. However, allowing that texts are open to interpretation need not result in a free-for-all of ad hoc, subjective impressions. It is necessary to say this because poststructuralist and postmodern positions are sometimes caricatured as if they collapse the world into a chaotic relativism and deny the reality of the physical world, or the possibility of objective truth. We don't see these as necessary concomitants of poststructuralism. It seems clear from the chaos of opinion on social media these days that there can be bizarre, perverse and contrarian interpretations of all sorts of media texts, although these can often be ascribed to an ideological motivation. Nonetheless, judgement can be applied on whether a given interpretation of a text, such as an advertisement, appears plausible or coherent to a fair-minded arbiter. Those judgements arise because the range of meanings cued by a given text are not infinite but to some degree must be constrained by the text in relation to its context and its readers. Interpretations of texts are not stable but might change over time as the cultural context changes. For example, we are all familiar with ads from the 1940s, 1950s and 1960s which to a modern sensibility can seem deeply offensive or simply deceitful for their racial and gender stereotyping and outright deceit, for example in American ads that had medical doctors endorsing cigarette brands for their health-enhancing properties.[12] Advertisements make fascinating social documents revealing the prevailing social prejudices, norms and power relations in cultures of the time.

The iconic 1985 Levi's 501 jeans ad, Laundrette,[13] is an example of an ad the meanings of which changed over time. At the time, this ad was the quintessence of advertising creativity, its star Nick Kamen the apotheosis of advertising icons, and the jeans, well, they broke the coolness dial and were an essential accessory to young folks wishing to be part of the zeitgeist. A decade later, the jeans, and the ad, and the people still wearing the jeans, were lame, corny and, well, old. The creative execution played on the prestige of American provenance and drew on a myth of 1950s America idealised in Hollywood movies (although the music track to the ad, Marvin Gaye's 'I Heard It Through The Grapevine',[14] was released in 1968) to suggest implicitly that denim jeans meant youth, glamour, sexiness, America and freedom. A decade later, American prestige had fallen away, young people no longer remembered iconic jeans-wearing movie actors like Marlon Brando and James Dean, and denim jeans simply meant leisure wear. The original campaign (by BBH) was extraordinarily successful because the ad crystallised a popular cultural sentiment and expressed it in a powerfully condensed form.[15] Over time, the meaning of denim jeans and of American provenance changed, and hence so did the meaning of the ad as construed by a new generation of young people. The trajectory of Levi's 501 jeans' sales followed the trajectory of the campaign as a cultural product. It was read one way in 1985, and a decade later a new audience with a different frame of cultural reference read it as a different ad.

At this point, we want to say a little more about Genette's ideas and how they might help us understand the ways in which advertisements are read and interpreted.

GENETTE AND THE TEXTUALITY OF ADVERTISEMENTS

Genette's work on paratexts is part of his theory of transtextuality, which built on his earlier work *Palimpsests: Literature in the Second Degree.* Transtextuality refers to a form of criticism that transcends the text to consider all the ways in which a text is connected to other texts. Genette's sub-categories of transtextuality are intertextuality, paratextuality, metatextuality, architextuality and hypertextuality, and he uses many sub-sub-categories of each. These categories overlap and are nuanced subtly in Genette's literary analysis. Metatextuality refers to implicit or explicit commentary on one text in another, such that the reference to the other text is understood but not necessarily explicit. Architextuality refers to the genre classification of a text which affects the reader's reception based on their assumptions about the genre to which it belongs. Hypertextuality refers to a text that refers to an earlier text (the hypotext) and extends or adapts the genre boundaries of the earlier text, cueing alternative readings, as in parody, prequel or pastiche.[16] We are mainly concerned for our purposes with paratextuality and intertextuality.

As we note in the previous chapter, Genette's paratextuality builds on Julia Kristeva's[17] ideas about intertextuality. Intertextuality refers to the interdependence of texts, the idea that no text can be meaningful independently of other texts. Just as a phoneme needs other phonemes to form a meaningful word, texts require other texts to be meaningful. Meaning is a relational construct, produced through language, in interaction. In literature, intertextuality can include plagiarism, allusion and quotation, and Genette emphasised that intertextuality can be implicit or explicit. This means, of course, that the interpretation depends on the reader's prior knowledge of other texts, or lack thereof. Part of the act of producing meaning entails connecting texts, and contexts.

For example, advertising slogans such as 'Just Do It';[18] Taste the Rainbow;[19] Finger Lickin' Good;[20] Where's the Beef?;[21] Red Bull Gives you Wings;[22] or 'Whassup?'[23] can only be fully understood by people who have the necessary cultural knowledge to connect the advertising strapline with its reference in wider culture in order to generate meaning. Understanding these examples demands a knowledge of idiomatic American English or slang and their use in advertising language, along with knowledge of the socio-cultural practices to which the slogans refer. These include licking one's fingers after eating 'fast' food without cutlery, taking part or competing in athletic training, and drinking 'energy' drinks. The slogans become meaningful though the audience's understanding of cultural practices of branding, advertising, eating fried chicken, drinking caffeinated drinks, and so on. An additional benefit of using idiomatic forms of address in ads is that they break through the formality of text to address us as if we were being addressed in the familiar way a friend might address us. Taste the Rainbow is a declarative instruction (or request) clearly meant for the reader of the ad, and is a far warmer way to connect with the audience than the announcement 'Please attend this ad for information about the confectionary brand, Skittles'.

We have noted that even simple declarative advertising texts require the reader to do some interpretive work, while more allusive texts demand more work. Far from being a failure in communication, creating cryptic ads which can be interpreted in different ways (or which can be deemed to have no meaning at all) can be strategically useful for advertisers (note Stefano Puntoni and colleagues' work on strategic polysemy that we also mentioned earlier in the book). We are socialised into the expectation that communications are saying something to us. When what they are saying is unclear or incoherent at first sight, the reader might be sufficiently intrigued to be drawn into the game of interpretation, enhancing the depth and duration of the reader's engagement with the ad, with concomitant positive effects on ad and brand recall and affect. Not only that, but when readers have to draw on their social knowledge in order to decode a meaning from the ad, this deepens the resonance of the ad for each individual, making it seem more relevant to the reader and embedding it within their life experience. Ads that we notice and think about are also often the ads we talk about to others, and these are the ads that become famous.

THE TWO-WAY EXCHANGE OF CULTURAL MEANING IN ADVERTISEMENTS

Sometimes, advertising slogans have passed into wider cultural usage, such as the Wendy's fast food chain slogan 'Where's the Beef?' which is an expression sometimes used to denote anything that is deemed lacking in substance. Other expressions move from social texts to advertising texts, such as 'Just Do It' which was attributed to a notorious American death row prisoner when he was asked if he had any last words, inspiring ad man Dan Wieden of Wieden+Kennedy to create the famous Nike slogan.[24] Budweiser's 'Whassup?' was based on a common greeting in

America, 'what's up?', adapted for, and amplified through, advertising, and which then passed back into non-advertising culture with its inclusion in established dictionaries.[25] In a sense, the makers of creative advertising, the ad agencies, act as cultural intermediaries, trading in and adding economic value to the signs, symbols and practices of popular culture.[26] They add this value through their vantage point at the nexus of commerce and culture, combining their insider knowledge of marketing and media processes, and their knowledge of consumers and consumption.[27]

A visual example of the advertising text both drawing from and inflecting wider cultural texts can be seen in the Coca-Cola Christmas ad image of a rotund, white-bearded man in a red jumpsuit representing the Western Christian legend of Santa Claus. This image was not invented by Coke's ad agency, it had been in cultural circulation earlier amongst other images of the mythical Santa Claus figure (a composite of local legend mixed with historical Christian figures such as Saint Nicholas), but it was adapted for Coke advertising in 1990 by artist Haddon Sundblom. Henceforth, this particular representation of Santa was amplified through the ad campaigns and became strongly associated with Coca-Cola for many years, such that the presence of the beverage was often not necessary for the idea of Coke to be invoked, just as audiences familiar with the Budweiser 'Whassup?' campaigns might think of the beer when they hear the phrase used without connection to the beer.

In another example of meanings passing from advertising to wider consumer culture, Diamond brand De Beers didn't so much as borrow from consumer culture as invent it when their 1980s ad campaign popularised the idea that men should commit two months' salary to their engagement ring.[28] What is sometimes claimed to be the best advertising slogan ever invented, 'Diamonds Are Forever', had been created by copywriter Mary Francis Geraghty for an A.J. Ayer campaign in the 1940s.[29] De Beers realised that to sell more diamonds, they had to attach them to a powerful cultural institution, so, through their advertising, they introduced the idea that diamonds signified love, and marriage was the occasion that had to be marked by a diamond gift. The idea of two months' salary cleverly played into ideas of social status by introducing a competitive element – the more expensive the diamond given and received, the higher the status and prestige of both giver and receiver. Diamonds became layered with meaning thanks to advertising paratexts, and the advertising influence tapped into and amplified wider social discourses and practices. De Beers' campaigns even enjoyed success in some countries that previously had no tradition of diamond giving for betrothal, especially, Japan.[30]

We can see from these examples how brand paratexts can have a mobile quality as cultural texts, oscillating between commercial and non-commercial culture and sometimes changing in their meanings over time. Advertisements that amplify certain images, music, slogans, ideas or symbols successfully to large audiences take the brand along with them in a journey into popular consumer culture. The brand persists as a silent intertext when these symbolic forms of communication extend into common consciousness and are repeated outside of the advertising text, in TV show scripts, media articles, comedy routines and everyday conversation.

THE HIERARCHY OF PRIMARY AND SECONDARY TEXT

As we note earlier, the influence of formalist literary criticism can be seen in some of the literary research into advertisements that we have mentioned. The advertising text is treated as complete and self-contained work, the meaning of which resides solely within it without reference to social texts outside the work. Such formalist analyses would focus on a 'close' reading of the formal structures of the advertising text regarding, say, figures of speech, metaphor and symbols. While providing a rich analysis that reveals the complexity of advertising texts, such analyses do not provide an adequate explanation of the ways in which the meaning of signs and symbols can change over time and flow between social texts such as advertisements, and everyday culture. In traditional literary criticism the novel, poem, libretto of a musical production or script of a play are treated as primary texts in the sense that they hold a unique authority as a source of the meaning of the work. But what does this mean when applied to brands? If a brand is understood as a primary text, to what extent can it claim ontological priority over its paratexts?

Genette argued that the secondary texts or paratexts that are conventionally treated as if they are peripheral to the primary text are far more important to the way a text is read and interpreted than conventionally supposed. Indeed, he suggested that a text is brought into being through its paratexts. A paratext acts as a threshold of entry into the primary text, and therefore influences the narrative direction the reader takes through the text, framing its meaning. As Genette elaborated, a text itself 'rarely appears in its naked state, without the reinforcement and accompaniment of a certain number of productions ... like an author's name, a title, a preface, illustrations ... precisely in order to present it ... and its consumption, in the form ... of a book'. It is through its paratexts that '... a text makes a book of itself and proposes itself as such to its readers, and more generally to the public' (p. 261).[31] He gives a striking example: '... reduced to its text alone and without the help of any instructions for use, how would we read Joyce's Ulysses if it were not called Ulysses?' (p. 262).

James Joyce's famously obtuse work challenges the paradigmatic literary conventions of the modernist novel: readers are invited by its title to think of it as a reworking of Homer's epic poem, yet much of the content engages with lowbrow bawdiness and self-parody. It is a text that is difficult enough to navigate with its associated paratexts but would be hardly possible to do so without them. The paratexts are a route into the text, but Genette's scheme does not allow that a primary text's paratexts can become the dominant source of meaning, thereby subverting the primary/secondary text hierarchy.

We have already referred in passing to Genette's division of paratexts into those that are included within the physical work and those that are exterior to it. Peritexts are contained within the literary work, and include footnotes, prefaces, titles and chapter headings, cover blurbs, images, typeface and sleeve notes. Epitexts are texts that refer to the book but are exterior to it, and include published reviews, interviews with the author, the author's early drafts and margin notes, advertisements for the book, compilations, serialisations, dramatisations, parodies or critiques. It is easy to imagine how a review of a book or movie can become the dominant reading for those who do not read or see the original work. There are many of us who, like Chris, a character in Arthur Miller's play *All My Sons*, read the book review section of the weekend newspaper but seldom read the books under review, Chris's justification being that he did so to 'keep abreast of my ignorance'. The idea of the popular meaning of a book being defined by its paratexts echoes Berger and Luckman's[32] famous example of a socially constructed reality. As each person passes on their opinion of the book, it is reinterpreted and re-articulated, until the account in circulation bears little connection with the original work. Paratexts, then, are liminal entities – they can change the meaning of the primary text to which they refer. They might define the meaning of a work for people who form an opinion from prior paratexts they encounter, they might frame the way the work is read for people who, say, see an advertisement for the work and then buy and read it, or they might change the meaning if a person reads a work and then changes their understanding of it after reading a review or commentary that makes them look at the work in a different light.

But, even if an epitext can cue the dominant conventional meaning of its primary text, it is hard to see how the hierarchy of primary/secondary text has been subverted in the case of a literary text, since, whether one has read it or not, there is a book, containing a lot of words in a carefully designed order, to which the peritetextual elements are narratively peripheral. However influential over popular opinion a published review may have been, it cannot gainsay the fact that there is a book on which some readers will form a different opinion to the popular one shared by people who have only read the review. We could say the same, though, of a brand, except the brand is a far more complex material entity than a book, consisting, say, of factories, products, production machinery, intellectual property, offices, employees and a history. It is, perhaps, more intuitively appealing to say that the meaning of a brand is given by its paratexts, than to say so of a book. As with the literary work, we could perhaps say there is an ontological priority to the brand/book in relation to its paratexts. A more difficult question to answer is whether the primary text of the book/brand is more important or influential in its meaning than its paratexts. We will come back to this problem in the following chapter.

PARATEXTUAL BRANDED CONTENT

Extending the metaphor of the text to electronic and other non-literary media (whether digital, paper, megaphone or anything else) Genette's ideas have been widely applied in literary, media, film and TV studies, as we've noted, examining such phenomena as movie trailers and promotions, TV channel interstitials or 'idents', and transmedia storytelling, a technique from film entertainment that entails telling episodes of the story on different media platforms. The creative and cultural industries use many forms of paratext to promote their productions. Book publishers, for example, have evolved into 'content machines' according to Michael Bhaskar[33] who writes of the complex forms of 'paracontent' in which publishers now trade. For Bhaskar, paracontent is a reflexive form of advertisement that advertises itself as much as it advertises another entity, such as the brand. As epitextual content relating to a (perhaps notional) primary text, paracontent assumes its own textual authority. It does not need the primary text to exist, just as someone can enjoy an advertisement without knowing, or caring, what is being advertised.

Digital communication is increasing the types of promotional content that can be created. TV channel interstitials are essentially short advertising spots[34] that are often inserted in the interstices between programming, titles, channel announcements and spot advertising. For example, many promotional interstitials of sponsored TV shows are placed after the title sequence, but before the action begins, and after the action ends at an interval, but before the commercial break. The term interstitial has been co-opted by web advertisers to describe pop-up ads that cover the whole screen rather than just part of it[35] and that are placed between editorial content. Ident is a term usually used to describe the TV channel logo video that is played in most intervals between content. UK terrestrial channel, Channel 4, has become well known for the creative quality of its idents, some of which are displayed on its website.[36] There are, incidentally, new types of digital advertisement evolving all the time, such as the ephemeral ads on platforms such as TikTok which are time-sensitive and disappear unless the viewer responds immediately to the ad. These and many other evolving, hybrid promotional forms of media content might cue a particular interpretation of a media production such as a movie or TV show, but how might such vehicles inflect the meaning of non-media brands?

We suggest, firstly, that the distinction between a media brand such as a movie production and a non-media brand such as a car, a retail supermarket or a chocolate snack need not be important for our analysis. We have already seen that all brands can become movie stars if they feature in video productions. Under media convergence, every brand can act like a media brand, whether it is Aldi, BMW or comparethemarket.com. If creative advertising ever was salesmanship in print,[37] it isn't any more. Bhaskar's concept of paracontent seems to express the way that creative advertising communication has spun off its axis to become a branch of the creative and cultural industries. Media brands, like literary works, have a text that commands some authority, at least for some of the audience, as the Wachowski brothers found when they pushed the limits of transmedia storytelling to kill off Morpheus, protagonist of the *Matrix* movie trilogy, in a computer game.[38] In contrast, non-media consumer brands have materiality, history, and so on, but there is no authoritative text: there is simply a Russian doll of paratexts: inside each, is another. Where the primary text ought to be, there is a vacuum that must be filled. This is what we mean when we suggest that the primary text of the brand is notional – it is the sum of its paratexts.

This gives a slightly different nuance to the relation of primary text with paratext that holds with literary works or media brands. The brand exists as a substantive entity and the limits of its meaning must in principle be bounded by the material facts appertaining to the brand – is it a shoe or a hat? Is it identified with a country, a region, a town, a person? Does it have colour schemes, dimensions, a unique design? But in spite of the material facts of the brand, its meaning is not bounded by reference to a definitive primary work.

SUBVERTING THE HIERARCHY OF PRIMARY AND SECONDARY BRAND TEXT

Melissa Aronczyk[39] suggests that brand paratexts can subvert the hierarchical relation between primary and secondary text by assuming a meaning that is dominant and, in some cases, unconnected to the brand. This departs from the assumed hierarchy of meaning we discuss above in which the primary text retains a dominant relationship to the paratext. As we mentioned earlier, a lot of people are familiar with advertising images, characters or catchphrases without necessarily having viewed the ads and without necessarily being familiar with the brand. For example, Mercedes-Benz has been an icon of cinema and popular songs for many years.[40] How many people have learned the meaning of the brand from movies and popular culture who have never driven the car and never will, and whom perhaps would not recognise a Mercedes car if they saw it?

For that matter, how many of the audience for *Casino Royale*, the 2006 James Bond movie release, had never heard of Omega watches before Bond himself explained that he was wearing one instead of his usual Rolex?[41] Of course, this is an example of a very particular type of promotional communication, movie product placement, and some Bond afficionados were appalled by such crass commercial exploitation of their cinematic hero.[42] The thing is, *Casino Royale* was the fourth highest-grossing movie of 2006,[43] and many in the movie's vast worldwide audience would not know that Bond usually wore Rolex watches in Ian Fleming's books. Omega, then, became the Bond watch for millions of people. Non-media brands, then, have seen the value of becoming entertainment properties. Through such exposure, new meanings can be inscribed and re-inscribed into the empty or ambiguous space of the brand.[44] A brand like Omega already has a cultural presence through its proprietorial designs, its narratives, its history, but these meanings are relatively mobile and subject to the authority and immediacy of new paratexts, and to the readings of new audiences.

Movie product placement has moved on since advertising boards were conspicuously placed in the street scenes of silent movies. Like advertising more generally, product (or brand) placement isn't just one technique, it is many.[45] For example, the brand might feature visually in the scene, and it might be written into the script as well, as in the Bond example above. It might even be there serendipitously as a hurriedly supplied scene prop and not pre-arranged and paid for by the brand.[46] The volume and rapidity of the TV content production cycle means that only a small proportion of brands appearing therein are there by contracted arrangement. Very often, a scene is planned and the set dresser or props manager is charged with finding the necessary props by next morning. Most brands understand that presence in any entertainment medium can invest the brand with the reflected prestige and allure of movies and films (not to mention novels, popular songs and stage plays). The wealthier brands can pay to be involved in productions as they develop, even to the extent of influencing the way they feature in the production.

SOCIAL MEDIA PARATEXTS

Social media content can also exert a powerful paratextual influence. Elon Musk's tweets have been known to make or break bitcoin millionaires, such is the authority with which Musk's often impulsive social media content is read, while footballer Christiano Ronaldo's removal of the sponsor Coca-Cola's bottles from his desk during a TV interview at the 2020 European Championships was reported to have knocked US$4 billion off the fizzy drink brand's market capitalisation in the space of half an hour[47] during which the clip of the incident went viral. Ronaldo (with his 303 million, and rising, Instagram followers)[48] is well known to be obsessed with his fitness, as befitting one of the world's most successful sportspeople, so it is hardly surprisingly that he prefers water to notoriously unhealthy carbonated drinks. Insiders pointed out that the share market as a whole dropped just prior to his notorious TV interview so it was likely that the fall in price of Coca-Cola shares was not connected to the Ronaldo incident, and besides, the bottle of water he held up as a healthier alternative was also a Coke brand. What the incident demonstrated was Ronaldo's vast media reach and the power of incidental digital content to assume the authority of the primary text, at least for a time.[49]

As an aside, although it is not always true that any publicity is good publicity, it would also be wrong to assume that brands ought necessarily to be dismayed by a negative media paratext. Nike, for example, was subject to calls for a brand boycott and a social media backlash when it used former NFL star and anti-racism activist Colin Kaepernick in a 2018 campaign called Dream Crazy, with some reports even claiming that their sales and share price suffered as a result.[50] However, it turned out that Nike's assessment of the progressive mentality of their key market was as sure-footed as usual, and the ad was subsequently acclaimed as a success, winning a coveted Emmy award.[51]

CONCLUDING COMMENTS

Our aim in this chapter has been to try to clarify our usage of the metaphor of the text and to show some of the ways it can be applied to advertising. It is important to state that the textual metaphor includes but is not limited to, the copy, script or type font in an advertisement, and extends to any part of the ad, including the music and visual imagery, all of which elements can be understood as symbols to be actively read by an interpreting audience. We hope we have also clarified the idea that the meaning of a text is not wholly encoded into the work itself but extends beyond the work. In other words, the meanings of brand texts are culturally mediated, they are produced through language in interaction by readers who interpret the meaning of the text in the light of their cultural knowledge. The borders of text and meaning are not located within the work itself but are delimited by their paratexts. The chapter has also discussed the relation between text and paratext, and we have touched on a key assumption of the book, namely that brands can be understood as notional primary texts that are, like the primary texts of literature, brought into being by their paratexts. We have suggested that brands, and in particular, non-media brands, have an ambiguous or empty character as media texts. The paratexts that connect to them can inscribe meanings into them, subverting the hierarchy of primary and secondary text. We develop this phenomenon, and other aspects of the brand as a locus of cultural meaning, in Chapter 4.

NOTES

1.   Genette's works on paratexts were not published in English translations until a decade or so after they were published in France. Genette published *Seuils*

in Paris in 1987: Marie Maclean translated the introduction for New Literary History in 1991, and the full English translation of *Seuils* was published as *Paratexts: Thresholds of Interpretation* in 1997 (translated by Jane Lewin). Genette's earlier work, *Palimpsests: Literature in the Second Degree*, published in 1982, is considered an important precursor to *Paratexts: Thresholds of Interpretation*.

2. Frank C. Pierson, *The Education of American Businessmen* (1959), McGraw Hill, gives an account of the impact of the Ford and Carnegie reports into American business education, the (possibly unintended) consequence of which was to create a bias for quantitative research based on a realist ontology. This has resulted in deep confusion in the field about how research findings inform managerial practice, not to mention profound divisions between various ostensibly incompatible research traditions in business schools.

3. Wolfgang Iser, The reading process: A phenomenological approach, *New Literary History*, 3(2), On Interpretation (Winter, 1972) 279–299, 279.

4. Catherine Harbour, At the desire of several persons of quality and lovers of musick: Pervasive and persuasive advertising for public commercial concerts in London 1672–1749. *Journal of Marketing Management*, 33(13–14) (2017) 1170–1203. DOI: 10.1080/0267257X.2017.1380687.

5. For a broader perspective on the marketing of concerts at the time see Catherine Harbour, The marketing of concerts in London 1672–1749. *Journal of Historical Research in Marketing*, 12(4) (2020) 449–471. DOI: 10.1108/JHRM-08-2019-0027.

6. For an account of Holloway's marketing techniques see: https://www.fulltable.com/vts/h/holl/b.htm

7. https://www.royalholloway.ac.uk/

8. For an account of Wedgwood's marketing magic see: https://thehustle.co/josiahwedgwood

9. See https://www.ozy.com/true-and-stories/the-marketing-genius-of-samuel-colt/32522/

10. And an academic article here comparing Barnum with a modern-day equivalent, Simon Cowell: Stephen Brown and Chris Hackley, The Greatest Showman on Earth: Is Simon Cowell P.T. Barnum reborn? *Journal of Historical Research in Marketing*, 4(2) (2012) 290–308. DOI: 10.1108/17557501211224467.

11. Jacques Derrida, *Structure, Sign and Play in the Discourse of Humanities. Writing and Difference*, trans. A. Bass (1978), University of Chicago Press.

12. There are many advertising history archives that make interesting viewing, such as this one at Duke University: https://repository.duke.edu/dc?utf8=%E2%9C%93&q=cigarette&search_field=all_fields

13. Laundrette, by Levi's and BBH, on YouTube: https://www.youtube.com/watch?v=Q56M5OZS1A8

14. https://www.youtube.com/watch?v=hajBdDM2qdg

15. https://www.hitc.com/en-gb/2021/05/06/levis-advert-nick-kamen/

16. Sayyed Ali Mirenayat and Elaheh Soofastaei, Gerard Genette and the categorization of textual transcendence. *Mediterranean Journal of Social*

Sciences, 6(5) (2015) 533–537. DOI:10.5901/mjss.2015.v6n5p533. Available at: https://www.academia.edu/18894684/Gerard_Genette_and _the_Categorization_of_Textual_Transcendence?email_work_card=view -paper

17. Julia Kristeva, *Desire in Language: A Semiotic Approach to Literature and Art* (1980), Columbia University Press.

18. Nike's famous slogan coined in 1987 by Dan Wieden of ad agency Wieden+Kennedy (see https://www.creativereview.co.uk/just-do-it-slogan/)

19. A confectionary brand called Skittles – with an ad here: https://www .youtube.com/watch?v=B4kwXcfv7Is

20. Kentucky Fried Chicken's famous slogan since the 1950s: https://www .creativereview.co.uk/its-finger-lickin-good-slogan-kfc/

21. Wendy's Burger's 'Where's the Beef?' slogan is probably more famous than the burger brand. See the original 1984 TV ad here: https://www.youtube .com/watch?v=Ug75diEyiA0

22. The global branding phenomenon based on the Red Bull energy drink.

23. 'Whassup?', of course, graduated from a 1999 Budweiser beer TV to the most reputable English language dictionaries. The ad can be seen here: https://www.youtube.com/watch?v=ikkg4NobV_w

24. Jeremy W. Peters, The birth of 'Just Do It' and other magic words (2009), *The New York Times*. https://www.nytimes.com/2009/08/20/business/ media/20adco.html

25. https://dictionary.cambridge.org/dictionary/english/wassup

26. See Anne M. Cronin, Regimes of mediation: Advertising practitioners as cultural intermediaries? *Consumption Markets & Culture*, 7(4) (2004) 349–369. DOI: 10.1080/1025386042000316315.

27. On the knowledge acquisition process for (pre-digital) advertising agencies, see Chris Hackley, The panoptic role of advertising agencies in the production of consumer culture. *Consumption Markets & Culture*, 5(3) (2002) 211–229. DOI: 10.1080/10253860290031640.

28. https://www.goodhousekeeping.com/life/money/a32609/two-months-salary -engagement-ring-rule-origin/

29. https://medium.com/4thought-studios/a-diamond-is-forever-but-its-value -isnt-c0c68052d016

30. https://www.theatlantic.com/international/archive/2015/02/how-an-ad -campaign-invented-the-diamond-engagement-ring/385376/

31. Genette and Mclean (1991), p. 261.

32. Peter L. Berger and Thomas Luckman, *The Social Construction of Reality: A Treatise in the Sociology of Knowledge* (1966), Penguin Books.

33. Michael Bhaskar, *The Content Machine: Towards a Theory of Publishing From the Printing Press to the Digital Network* (2013), Anthem Press.

34. https://www.studiodaily.com/2009/08/interstitialsa%E2%80%9Aa-aa%E2 %80%9Aa-big-word-for-short-spots/

35. https://www.studiodaily.com/2009/08/interstitialsa%E2%80%9Aa-aa%E2 %80%9Aa-big-word-for-short-spots/

36. Channel 4's 2021 ident gallery: https://theident.gallery/menu_section _channel4.php

37. In John E. Kennedy's famous expression.
38. Described by Henry Jenkins in *Convergence Culture: Where Old and New Media Collide* (2006), New York University Press.
39. Melissa Aronczyk, Portal or police? The limits of promotional paratexts. *Critical Studies in Media Communication*, 34(2) (2017) 111–119. DOI: 10.1080/15295036.2017.1289545.
40. See a video of rock icon Janis Joplin singing the anthem to consumption, 'Oh Lord Won't You Buy Me a Mercedes-Benz' (1970): https://www.youtube.com/watch?v=Qev-i9-VKlY
41. https://blog.hollywoodbranded.com/blog/james-bond-product-placement -the-definitive-timeline-of-brands-in-bond
42. For an entertaining account of Bond movie placement deals see: https:// www.bbc.com/culture/article/20151001-does-bonds-product-placement-go -too-far
43. https://www.boxofficemojo.com/release/rl3428484609/
44. See Stephen Brown, *Brands and Branding* (2016), Sage.
45. See Rungpaka Amy Tiwsakul, Chris Hackley and Isabelle Szmigin, Explicit, non-integrated product placement in British television programmes. *International Journal of Advertising*, (Q1) 24(1) (2005) 95–111. DOI: 10.1080/02650487.2005.11072906.
46. See Chris Hackley and Rungpaka Amy Hackley née Tiwsakul, Unpaid product placement: The elephant in the room in the UK's new paid-for product placement market. *International Journal of Advertising*, 31(4) (2012) 703–718. DOI: 10.2501/IJA-31-4-703-718.
47. https://www.business-standard.com/article/sports/footballer-cristiano -ronaldo-knocks-off-4-billion-from-coca-cola-s-value-121061600680_1 .html
48. The 303 million followers figure for @christiano on Instagram is correct as of 23 June 2021.
49. According to Mark Ritson it also demonstrated that marketers can't agree on anything: https://www.marketingweek.com/mark-ritson-ronaldo-damage -coke-brand/
50. For example, this *Guardian* report: https://www.theguardian.com/sport/ 2018/sep/04/nike-controversial-colin-kaepernick-campaign-divisive
51. https://www.theguardian.com/sport/2019/sep/16/nikes-dream-crazy-advert -starring-colin-kaepernick-wins-emmy

4. Paratexts and the meaning of the brand

INTRODUCTION

In this chapter we want to discuss the idea that brands can be understood as deeply ambiguous entities the meanings of which are mediated through advertising paratexts. The suggestion that a brand image is a deeply ambiguous or empty space into which meanings can be inscribed tends to be pushed out of mainstream brand management conversations[1] in favour of a rather reified notion of the brand image as something that has an 'essence', a 'core' of values and associations, even a 'soul', all of which contribute to the vague notion of brand equity.[2] The reification of the brand image, and the way it is received and interpreted by consumers and the world at large, is animated by the idea that the meaning of a brand can be controlled by brand management. There can be no doubt that there is material substance to brands, but the brand image, the brand's cultural meaning, can be understood as an ambiguous and contested space.[3] Brand meaning can evolve and change and, of course, is open to manipulation, which, after all, is the point of brand management. We suggest that conceptualising a brand as a vehicle for meaning, rather than as a bundle of more or less essential associations and attributes, has quite different implications for brand management and cultural and consumer policy.

THE AMBIGUOUS BRAND

The inherent ambiguity of some consumer brands can be seen from the strikingly different creative approaches to their advertising over the years. For example, the first Coca-Cola ad, in 1886, featured a strapline exhorting the 'Delicious, refreshing, exhilarating and invigorating'[4] medicinal qualities of the beverage. The medicinal properties of the drink were subsequently set aside in favour of appeals that broadened the market. Perhaps the most significant move in the brand's history was when it responded to stories that American troops abroad in the Second World War were missing the drink because it reminded them of home by sending shiploads of free product. The brand (by this time popularly known as 'Coke') subsequently became a symbol of home for service personnel, and, by association, a symbol of American values.[5]

In the 1970s, the emphasis of Coke advertising had shifted away from patriotic nationalism towards multi-ethnic inclusivity with the 'I'd like to buy the world a Coke' 'Hilltop' ad.[6] Along the way, Coke advertising set the gold standard in creative elaborations around the brand image, developing new paratexts to inflect the meaning of the ambiguous brand image. According to a 1961 TV ad, Coke helped you to stay slim,[7] it became a Christmas drink in the 1930s[8] (as we touched on in the previous chapter), while many other Coke ads play up the cooling properties of the drink as hot weather refreshment, or as an accessory to heightened sporting or social status.[9] Another long-running ad equated Coke with happiness,[10] and a more recent Chinese ad promoted Coke as a symbol of family, good fortune and prosperity,[11] amongst many other creative interpolations of the brand. Coca-Cola has engaged in high-profile sponsored tie-ins with a bewildering variety of events, celebrities and causes, inserting the brand into a huge variety of cultural spaces with vast audience reach, including being a major sponsor of the Olympic Games since 1928.[12]

The ideas implied in Coca-Cola advertising are strategically vague, evincing Stefano Puntoni and colleagues' idea of purposeful polysemy.[13] Ambiguous ads reflect the ambiguity of the brand, into which many different (and sometimes mutually contradictory) meanings can be inserted without apparently disturbing the consumer's sense of order in the world. The truth about consumers is that we don't think very deeply about brands, and, in any case, memories are short and humans are not very alert to logical inconsistency. This does not mean that what a brand does with its advertising doesn't matter – there is art and craft to creative advertising that sells, but the key principle is to create advertising that people enjoy, and which doesn't damage the brand. Segmenting defined market audiences and targeting them with univocal messages may have its place in brand communication management, but full control of the brand image by its management is neither useful nor possible.[14]

The variety, volume and colour of Coke advertising kept its market share atop of its competitors by keeping it salient, that is present and current, amongst the broad audience who might buy a Coke a few times a year when it is offered in a restaurant or refreshment kiosk. Alongside the iconic creativity in Coke's rich advertising history there has also been the occasional controversy, such as the Superbowl 2014 ad that portrayed 'America the Beautiful' being sung by ethnically diverse performers (including a gay male couple with a baby) in their native language, and which received a negative social media backlash from some white Americans who rejected its values.[15] Perhaps this ad divided Coke's older, conservative audience and its younger more politically progressive audience. By then, Coke was promoting a reflexive advertising strategy it called Content 2020[16] to reflect the participative instincts of Millennial consumers.

Brand meanings are invariably contested and provisional – brands look out into popular culture to see what ideas might be turned to the brand's purposes. These ideas usually do not originate in advertising but, rather, advertising amplifies them and links them to the brand. In the previous chapter we discussed examples of the cultural curation indulged in by brands and ad agencies (appropriation seems too loaded a word), with examples of Coke and Santa Claus, Budweiser and Levi's. These examples are of course dated, and any outrage they might have stirred in the general public would easily be ignored by the brand. In contrast, today, there are sensitivities to be negotiated, such as in our 'America the Beautiful' example from 2014, or in the notorious 2017 Kendall Jenner Pepsi ad.[17] When this happens, though, we suggest that it is more likely to be a failure of creativity or strategy (or, in the Pepsi example, miscasting, a bad script, unfortunate timing, or bad luck) than a reflection of the violation of essential brand values.

While the brand image and meaning are malleable there is also a symbolic casing, a superstructure that provides an essential sense of continuity so that people are clear about which brand is advertising, usually represented by a visual identity, and sometimes accompanied, at least for a time, by a slogan, an actor or a tune. For example, in the case of Coke the visual identity that links all its ads consists of the logo and colour scheme, the bottle (not introduced until 1916, by which time the brand had been in existence for 30 years) and of course the recipe and flavour. These elements amount to distinctive brand assets (in Byron Sharp's term, of whom, more below) that provide a foundation for countless creative iterations around the malleable meaning of the brand.

THE EVOLUTION OF BRAND MEANINGS IN POPULAR CULTURE

The history of Coca-Cola advertising is a useful record of how, over a long period, a brand created entertaining content for a broad audience that gave it a presence in popular culture, keeping it relevant and maintaining its place in public consciousness. This was the work of high budget, expensively produced advertising that was strategically and creatively astute, but the effect was prosaic – it kept the brand in people's minds and that helped to maintain its dominant market share. Ultimately, branding performs a pretty simple function, and it might be instructive to look at an example that is often claimed to be the first consumer brand of the modern era, Proctor and Gamble's Ivory soap.[18] The soap had the brand name Ivory (invented by Harley Proctor who was the founder's son) trademarked in 1879, as Proctor was farsighted in realising that naming a commodity held commercial advantages. Naming acts as a mnemonic aid,[19] and subsequent additions of a colour scheme and packaging enhanced the mnemonic effect, as did the straplines subsequently added to the packaging of '99 44/100% Pure' and 'It Floats'. These were not only visual elaborations on the branding but conceptual flourishes that added more layers to the brand meaning. The paratexts provided new points of entry into the brand, based on its claimed technical qualities, and its physical properties (the soap that floats).

The decisions on brand name and visual identity were creative but arbitrary – Proctor could have come up with different ideas. Indeed, when one looks at brand histories, a great many now iconic branding phenomena were serendipitous, arbitrary or accidental, such as the choice of brand name for Apple or Adidas, the Nike Swoosh[20] logo and many other brand elements. Adi (or Adolf) Dassler no doubt hoped that the athlete his Adidas brand sponsored and who wore his running shoes would win a medal at the 1936 Berlin Olympics, but he cannot have anticipated that Jesse Owens would win four gold medals in front of Adolf Hitler. Nike founders Phil Knight and Bill Bowerman took the same marketing path as Dassler by sponsoring the brand's first track athlete, more than 30 years later. Running legend Steve Prefontaine (also coached by Bowerman) boosted Nike's brand's appeal and credibility until his tragic early death at the age of 24.[21] Prefontaine made running cool, and, by association, performed a similar service for the brand. His persona grew bigger than the sport and, consequently, Prefontaine also helped grow the sport[22] as a whole by motivating more people to take up running. Prefontaine's personality was spiky and confrontational at times, he challenged authority and whatever he did or said became news, and the sometimes confrontational but socially progressive tone of Prefontaine's media persona still infuses much Nike advertising today.

The histories of Nike and many other prominent brands suggest that the cultural meaning of brands is not set down in a document by head office and imposed on consumers, but is, rather, something that evolves, filtered through cultural events, and is articulated through, and shaped by, the paratexts that emerge from the brand. The management of these paratexts may be astute and self-aware at times, the brand's evolution is not an accident, but it is not fully controlled either. Rather, brand management works with the ambiguity of the brand.

NIKE'S ADVERTISING REVOLUTION

Nike's 1987 Revolution ad[23] used the Beatles' protest song (released in 1968) to invest Nike Air shoes with a revolutionary frisson – an absurd proposal, on the face of it, for a shoe, and an affront to many Beatles fans who felt that the idealism of the song (and that of its composer John Lennon) was tainted by its association with a cynical commercial behemoth, as Alan Bradshaw and Linda Scott explain in their book, *Advertising Revolution*.[24] Indeed, the use of the music was an affront to the surviving Beatles as well (Lennon was murdered in 1980) and the group sued Nike and their ad agency Wieden+Kennedy in a drawn-out legal process that was mutually settled after several years had passed and four versions of the ad had been released.[25]

As Bradshaw and Scott explain, the ad was seen as a watershed in branding and advertising. The Levi's 501s Laundrette ad we discussed previously, aired two years before Revolution, had shown how powerful a marriage popular songs and branding could be, creating cultural resonance for the brand (and a new audience for the songs). However, Laundrette didn't use Mavin Gaye's version of 'I Heard it Through The Grapevine', but a cover version sung by session singers.[26] Nike's Revolution campaign used the Beatles' original track, and it was this, as much as the use of the song itself, that created such an impact because The Beatles had vowed not to allow their music to be used in advertising. Even though the Nike ad was degrading the meaning of the song for commercial purposes, its use lent a frisson of cultural authenticity to the brand.

Just as Levi's Laundrette revived sales of Motown music, Revolution introduced the music of The Beatles to a new generation, and the music industry recognised the huge commercial advantages to be gained from 'selling out' their art to brands with open cheque books who wanted an entrée into the coolest quarters of popular culture. In the 1980s Nike had grown into a billion-dollar company but was still second in running shoe sales to Reebok. The Revolution ad reframed the intent behind the song. John Lennon wrote the song as a cry against the established order, but Nike showed the value to brands of stepping right into the most sensitive areas of popular debate. The use of popular songs in ads also created a mutual association that would linger long in the minds of audiences – when the Beatles' 'Revolution' or Gaye's 'Grapevine' were revived by the ads, the songs acted as paratextual advertisements for the brand. Memory for popular culture is short and the brand soon becomes identified with the cultural reference in the ad for the new generation of younger consumers. How many music-loving Gen Xers assumed that 'Revolution' was a Nike track until their parents told them about John Lennon?

Nike's more recent paratextual initiatives have also demonstrated considerable poise in tapping into a progressive and politically radical tone. The launch of their sports hijab in 2018[27] was greeted with calls to boycott Nike and accusations of tokenism, even from commentators who applauded the addition to their product line. A year later the product was apparently selling well,[28] and in 2020 the brand added additional lines in swimwear.[29] Another major foray into sensitive cultural areas was choosing former NFL star and anti-racism activist Colin Kaepernick to front its 2018 Dream Crazy advertising campaign.[30] This campaign generated heated reaction and the by now predictable calls to boycott Nike but, as Phil Knight was quoted, it didn't matter if the brand was hated by some as long as it was loved by more,[31] and after the initially negative reactions in the trade press Nike sales were boosted as a result.[32]

The paratextual media comment and UGC (User Generated Content) swirling around Nike was hugely conflicting but, in spite of the storm of controversy, the brand succeeded in two ways. Firstly, its judicious paratextual communications generated a firestorm of interest that kept the brand at the top of public conversation in the media and elsewhere. There may be such a thing as bad publicity, but for consumer brands there are usually positive effects of simply being remembered by large audiences.[33] Secondly, the tone and themes of its advertising were astutely judged. The brand took on a role as social activist and that chimed with its core market, and the angry conservative voices against the brand gave this meaning its authenticity. When some consumers posted videos burning their Nike items with the hashtag #boycottnike, Nike produced its own video advising consumers how to burn their Nike products safely. Let's remind ourselves that we are talking about sports shoes, or headwear, or shorts and vest outfits and tracksuits. To discuss such items as having meanings linked to seismic events of social and cultural history seems absurd on the face of it. The fact that we talk seriously about brands as social activists or as sources of powerful cultural moments speaks to the extraordinary power of advertising to invest inanimate objects with layers of cultural meaning.

PARATEXTUAL BRANDING AND CULTURE

Marketing anthropologist Douglas Holt's cultural branding[34] offers a useful counterpoint to mainstream brand management approaches in that it places the location of brand meaning in culture, rather than in brand head office. We feel that the idea of paratextuality is broadly consistent with the major principles of Holt's framework, although from a differing theoretical angle with attendant differences in nuance. Holt's anthropologically informed cultural branding approach explicitly rejects the 'mindshare model'[35] of brand management in favour of a model based on cultural activism.[36] 'Mindshare' refers to the idea that a brand can be conceived as a bundle of images and associations that differentiate it from competitor brands. The idea was popularised by Al Riess and Jack Trout[37] in their book, *Positioning: The Battle For Your Mind*. Riess and Trout's influential work plays into a paradigm of scientific management whereby organisational managers are held to operate like scientists, removed from consumers, who are the objects upon which they perform their ingenious manipulative interventions. The brand as cultural activist, in contrast, taps into and aligns itself with cultural events, causes and trends, inserting the brand into those cultural spaces through various paratextual devices including signage, advertising, social media content and sponsored events.

For Holt, the meaning of a brand resides not in the cognitive structures of an individual brain, but in the socially mediated interactions of language and communication. Holt's work assumed that brands and brand managers are themselves part of the consumer cultural world, so, as a consequence, brand managers need to understand their brand as it functions in the interactive spaces of consumer culture. Holt expresses the idea of brands as cultural entities, writing that 'Iconic brands beat the competition not just by delivering innovative benefits, services, or technologies, but by forging a deep connection with the culture. A brand becomes an icon when it offers a compelling myth.'[38] Holt argues that iconic brands do this by targeting cultural contradictions: 'The deepest source of tension in modern society is the disparity between national ideology and the average citizen's reality. When ideologies shift, myths become even more important, and in America, the most potent myths are depictions of rebels.' Steve Prefontaine was not just Nike's foremost sponsored athlete but an anti-establishment figure who lived a runner's lifestyle before running was popular or fashionable. He epitomises the brand image, and all the media coverage of Prefontaine in the 1970s, the urban myths around his persona, and his legendary running feats, all amounted to paratextual brand content when his association with Nike became known.

For Holt, brands should '... learn to target national contradictions instead of just consumer segments, create myths that make sense of confusing societal changes, and speak with a rebel's voice'. This analysis might be most suited to post-war American brand culture with its Coca-Cola, Marlboro cigarettes, Harley Davidson motorcycles and other brands that tap into transgressive notes and play on myths of masculinity or American exceptionalism. Our point here is that whatever a brand's meaning may be, it is articulated and mobilised through media and other paratexts. The notional primary text of the brand is a space that is filled with paratextual inflections. This has several implications for the way brands are managed.

A brand is more than its communications, but many mainstream brand management texts and consulting formulae reify the idea of the brand as if were a bundle of benefits and attributes decided and controlled by head office and intended to fill a well-defined space in the consciousness of target consumers (the 'mindshare' model of brand management, as Holt describes it). Mainstream managerial brand management textbooks tend to see advertising as a neutral channel through which brand management imposes its own image of the brand on to passive consumers. In contrast, if the brand image, its meaning to the public, is seen as an ambiguous space that is negotiated through and mediated by paratextual media content, there are different implications about how advertising and brand management strategy should be designed. That brands are ambiguous is not merely an abstract theoretical point, but a managerial axiom. To state the obvious, branding must make it easy for a consumer to recall and buy the brand. When someone has to buy something in a particular category, they will usually make a choice from three or four items, human working memory, time and energy for shopping being limited. Brands facilitate cognitive economy. The brands that are recalled the most easily by large numbers of people, and are convenient to buy, will generally sell the most. The best-recalled and best-selling brands in a market are usually the ones that spend most on advertising.[39] The best-recalled brands are often those that are most richly elaborated as cultural entities. In other words, they are heavily advertised in ways that keep the brand interesting and fun and, therefore, current and relevant for consumers.

There is some inertia in markets as increased market share becomes self-perpetuating, provided the advertising spend remains high to reassure the buyer that their purchase remains salient. In fact, a lot of advertising is about reassurance, not persuasion, as Andrew Ehrenberg and colleagues demonstrated[40] with their long-running research programme at South Bank University. The efficacy of Proctor's Ivory soap was not the point – of course it needed to do what was expected so it had to be good enough, but as with many commodities it is unlikely that there was a huge difference in performance between different versions of the same commodity. Even if there were, there is a powerful circular logic to successful branding, as Ehrenberg realised – it is the continued presence of striking advertising content that reassures customers they made the right choice. The most successful consumer brands remake their consumer cultural presence continuously. The important thing is that the brand paratexts they produce should inflect the brand meaning in ways that audiences find compelling.

PARATEXTUAL BRANDING AND BRAND GROWTH

We suggest that our paratextual perspective on brand advertising allows us to link brand management ideas that might superficially seem incompatible. In particular, the literary idea of the advertising paratext lends itself to theories of advertising as publicity and, similarly, to Byron Sharp's ideas of why some brands lead the market. Like Ehrenberg, Sharp argues that brands do not need to engage in a sales conversation with target consumers. Sharp suggests that brands should avoid targeting and segmentation strategies based on a narrow conception of the target market and, instead, focus on continually reinforcing the brand presence, its physical and mental availability (or salience), to all the consumers in a category[41] and beyond. One way of doing this is to make the brand and its advertising entertaining so that people enjoy it. Market share growth, for Sharp, comes from attracting new users into the brand's universe and making it easy for them to become consumers of the brand. Sharp rejects the overemphasis often placed on brand differentiation and consumer loyalty in favour of creating a set of distinctive assets that can be brought to the attention of a wide audience. The lynchpin of a brand's efforts to generate a set of distinctive assets is, of course, advertising, in one form or another.

Examples of brand paratexts that eschew targeting in favour of providing entertainment to a general audience include the BMW movies, Volvo's Epic Split, and the comparethemarket.com meerkats, all of which were discussed in Chapter 1. Examples such as these also demonstrate another insight that paratextuality brings to contemporary advertising. This is that the branding message needs to be neither explicit, nor sales oriented. Neither the BMW movies, Epic Split nor any of the meerkats content has an explicit sales orientation (although the meerkats were conceived to increase the brand's visibility in organic search). They are all designed to be fun for their own sake. People will watch and enjoy Epic Split even if they happen not to be a truck buyer for a major logistics company, and this category applies to perhaps 99.9% of the audience. The content operates as a brand intertext, broadening the brand's universe, elaborating on its cultural resonance and enhancing its market presence. When an ad becomes famous, it is not only customers who want to talk about it, but audiences who are looking for entertainment, employees, others in the supply chain, shareholders and business journalists and bloggers. If we accept Genette's proposal that primary texts are brought into being by their paratexts, then we can see theoretically how these media paratexts have such influence over the notional primary text of the brand, even though they lack most of the typical elements of a traditional sales-oriented advertisement.

Brands, then, can benefit from advertising that entertains audiences beyond existing category users. Seen as brand paratexts, advertisements inflect the meaning of a brand and give it an enhanced cultural presence. Genette showed that the paratext operates as an interpretive threshold through which the primary text is entered, cueing the way it is to be read: '... we are dealing in this case with a threshold ... between the text and what lies outside it, a zone not just of transition, but of transaction; the privileged site of a pragmatics and of a strategy ...'.[42] Brands are made more complex and interesting to consumers by the paratexts around them, generating new and different points of entry into the world of the brand.[43]

BUSINESS SCHOOL ORTHODOXY AND PARATEXTUAL BANDING

A work of literature, for Genette, evinces meanings that are not fixed by the author or the publisher, but interpreted by readers. When applied to advertising paratexts, this idea makes clear that brand meaning is not something that can be inserted into consumers' minds on the hypodermic model of advertising communication favoured in typical business school approaches. The idea that brand managers effectively operate as programmers channelling data to be processed by targeted consumers does not square with socio-cultural theories of how communications are received and interpreted. For example, cultural sociologist Stuart Hall rejected the linear model of communication in his 1973 work[44] on television audiences, suggesting that a dominant-hegemonic reading of television texts that simply accepts the meaning as intended by the author of the text was a relatively unusual occurrence because the decoding of broadcast messages by different audiences is conducted from differing cultural perspectives. A negotiated or oppositional reading of the text was just as likely, or more likely given the heterogeneity of audiences. This message still needed to be explained to business school advertising researchers over 20 years later with Stern's work critiquing the linear source-encoding-message-decoding-audience transmission model of communication[45] in 1994.[46]

There has been quite a long tradition of anthropologically inspired work on brands that business school orthodoxy has largely resisted. Holt's work on cultural branding is the most successful expression of this tradition, but way back in 1959 Sidney Levy noted the symbolic elements of marketing in an anthropology-inspired *Harvard Business Review*[47] piece. Levy's timing was unfortunate since the Ford and Carnegie reports on business education (mentioned in Chapter 2) were published the same year. These now notorious[48] reports might have been well intentioned but they criticised the rigour of American business education and shifted the direction of university business school research into a model that marginalised qualitative and cultural anthropological perspectives in favour of a 'hard' management science approach. The idea of meaning was usually considered too nebulous and subjective to be subject to the kind of quantitative research studies that were seen to legitimise the authority of business school knowledge.

Interest in anthropological and socio-cultural perspectives from business school academics revived in the 1980s and 1990s, although this area remains bracketed as consumer research rather than marketing. For example, cultural anthropologist Grant McCracken argued that marketing as a discipline entails the management not of brand equity or brand assets, but of brand meaning.[49] Against the prevailing ideology of segmentation, targeting and control of the message, researchers interested in brand meaning found themselves positioned as rebels or heretics. Another business anthropologist, Russ Belk, took consumer research further down a cultural perspective in his work that showed how ownership of goods was inherent to the construction of self and social identity,[50] thus providing a direct link between cultural anthropology and research into brand consumption.

David Glen Mick and Claus Buhl took a different angle of approach to understand how brands mean, with their meaning-based model of advertising informed by qualitative phenomenological interviews[51] with consumers. John Schouten and Jim Alexander[52] took their cue from the Chicago School of qualitative sociology and hung out with the consumption sub-culture they wanted to write about – a gang of motor-cyclists (fortunately the academics had their own bikes). Work such as these examples used predominantly qualitative methods to examine the ways in which consumers make sense of and use brands, consumption and advertising[53] in their everyday lives. Cultural anthropology is more acceptable as a method in business schools today, but it still meets resistance from researchers who see objectively verifiable and measurable scientific knowledge as the only legitimate goal of social research.

1980s ads like Revolution and Laundrette made clear that not only could advertising amplify and inflect cultural meanings in ways that placed brands squarely at the heart of pop culture, but brands could appear as natural allies alongside other ostensibly more authentic phenomena of consumer culture, such as movies, pop songs and artists. Indeed, brands can be seen as intrinsic features of popular culture, with all the coolness and fame of pop or movie stars. One does not need to invoke paratextual theory to talk about brands as cultural icons – all the studies mentioned above were able to do so without any help from Genette. We feel that paratextual theory and associated literary concepts can help to elaborate the description, understanding and theorisation of such phenomena. The examples we invoke have shown how various paratexts inscribed layers of cultural meaning into the ambiguous meaning of the respective brands.

CONCLUDING COMMENTS

Paratextual theory is in part a theory of meaning, and we have tried to offer some examples of how advertising paratexts frame and cue the consumer cultural meaning of brands. We have touched on some of the intellectual prejudices and ideological divisions that divide business school research and theorising, especially in the marketing area. Having made some of these points in the context of an ontological discussion about whether a brand is a source of meaning located in the interstices of communicative culture, or a bundle of associations located in the cognitive apparatus of individual consumers, we need to explore how these two perspectives fit with ideas about the nature and commercial purpose of advertisements. In Chapter 5 we return, then, to a fundamental question – how does advertising work? – in order to locate our paratextual perspective within the fundamental reason for advertising: selling.

NOTES

1. For an example of a branding text that addresses the ambiguity of brands, see Stephen Brown, *Brands and Branding* (2016), Sage. For an example of a more mainstream, essentialist approach to brands as bundles of attributes, see Kevin Lane Keller, *Strategic Brand Management: Building, Measuring and Managing Brand Equity*, 4th Edition (2012), Pearson.
2. Richard Rosenbaum-Elliott, Larry Percy and Simon Pervan discuss a number of definitions of brand equity in their *Strategic Brand Management*, 4th Edition (2018), Oxford University Press.
3. An in-depth research study into brand ambiguity was published by Stephen Brown, Pierre McDonagh and Clifford J. Shultz II, *Titanic*: Consuming the myths and meanings of an ambiguous brand. *Journal of Consumer Research*, 40(4) (2013) 595–614. http://www.jstor.org/stable/10.1086/671474
4. See https://medium.com/swlh/coca-cola-ads-and-the-evolution-of-creativity -in-advertising-b0655b3da780
5. As Doug Holt describes in his book, *How Brands Become Icons – The Principles of Cultural Branding* (2004), Harvard Business Review Press.
6. 'Hilltop', Coke, 1971: https://www.youtube.com/watch?v=1VM2eLhvsSM
7. Coke keeps you thin, 1961: https://youtu.be/8zTDbpxT8ZI
8. Santa Claus and Coca-Cola, 1931: https://www.coca-colacompany.com/ faqs/did-coca-cola-invent-santa

9. Lots of examples of Coke poster and magazine ads here from the advertising archives: https://www.advertisingarchives.co.uk/index.php?service=search &action=do_quick_search&language=en&q=coca+cola

10. Coke's 'happiness machine' ad, 2010: https://youtu.be/lqT_dPApj9U

11. Chinese Coke ad, 2020: https://youtu.be/q_DnIynjEGg

12. https://olympics.com/ioc/partners/coca-cola-mengniu

13. Stefano Puntoni, Joelle Vanhamme and Reuben Visscher, Two birds and one stone: Purposeful polysemy in minority targeting and advertising evaluations. *Journal of Advertising*, 40(1) (2011) 25–41. DOI: 10.2753/ JOA0091-3367400102.

14. For a discussion of the futility of trying to control a brand too tightly in the age of social media, see this feature piece about Coke advertising in *The Atlantic*: https://www.theatlantic.com/technology/archive/2016/01/things -you-cant-talk-about-in-a-coca-cola-ad/431628/

15. See https://www.latimes.com/entertainment/tv/showtracker/la-et-st-coca -cola-super-bowl-ad-stirs-controversy-20140203-story.html

16. See Coke's 'Content 2020' videos, widely available on video sharing websites including YouTube, e.g.: https://www.youtube.com/watch?v= LerdMmWjU_E

17. https://www.elle.com/uk/life-and-culture/culture/a32778311/kendall-jenner -pepsi-advert-black-lives-matter-protests/

18. Proctor and Gamble's brand history page for Ivory soap is here: https://ivory .com/our-heritage/

19. Anthropologist Marcel Danesi writes accessibly on the semiotics of brand-ing in *Brands* (2004), Routledge.

20. According to some stories, Apple was so called because Steve Jobs had worked in an apple orchard and wanted a brand name that stood out from the technical-sounding names of then rivals. Adidas came from the name of the proprietor, Adolf (Adi) Dassler, and the Nike Swoosh was commissioned from an art student for US$30. Word was that Phil Knight didn't like it but had to go with it because he needed a logo to compete with the famous three stripes of rival Adidas.

21. https://news.nike.com/news/40-years-of-prefontaine

22. https://www.cbc.ca/sports/olympics/summer/trackandfield/lasting-legend -of-running-icon-steve-prefontaine-1.4675852

23. See the first iteration of Nike's 1987 Revolution TV ad here: https://vimeo .com/89811766

24. See Alan Bradshaw and Linda Scott, *Advertising Revolution: The Story of a Song, From Beatles Hit to Nike Slogan* (2018), Repeater Books.

25. https://www.pophistorydig.com/topics/tag/nike-revolution-ad/

26. The release of the ad did revive interest in Gaye's music and the original was re-released, becoming a hit all over again: https://thisisnotadvertising .wordpress.com/2012/11/22/levis-501-the-story-behind-launderette/

27. See https://www.nbcnews.com/business/consumer/nike-s-hijab-prompts -backlash-boycott-praise-n733171

28. https://www.thenationalnews.com/lifestyle/fashion/the-nike-pro-hijab-has -become-one-of-the-world-s-most-popular-clothing-items-1.861183

29. https://www.sundaypost.com/fp/sports-giants-new-gear-for-muslim -women-has-the-swoosh-of-success/
30. See the first ad here: https://www.youtube.com/watch?v=-grjIUWKoBA
31. Quote in this academic analysis of Dream Crazy: https://medium.com/ swlh/just-buy-it-a-critical-analysis-of-nikes-dream-crazy-advertisement -campaign-169190f14a89
32. https://www.fastcompany.com/90399316/one-year-later-what-did-we-learn -from-nikes-blockbuster-colin-kaepernick-ad
33. One anecdotal example is that the environmental catastrophe and human tragedy of BP's 2010 oil spill in the Gulf was reported to have caused the brand's petrol sales to rise as more drivers pulled into BP filling stations, presumably an effect of the brand's media presence. In the longer term, for many reasons, the brand has survived, when for a time it looked as if it might not. https://www.adn.com/business-economy/energy/2018/07/16/ after-deepwater-horizon-a-new-bp-emerges/
34. See https://www.culturalstrategygroup.com/
35. See another Holt 2003 article, How to build an iconic band, in *Market Leader*, full text here: https://www.researchgate.net/publication/267922691 _How_to_Build_an_Iconic_Brand
36. For a fuller exposition of this technique see Douglas Holt and Douglas Cameron, *Cultural Strategy: Using Innovative Ideologies to Build Breakthrough Brands* (2010), Oxford University Press.
37. Al Riess and Jack Trout, *Positioning: The Battle for your Mind* (2001), McGraw Hill.
38. Douglas Holt, What becomes an icon most? *Harvard Business Review* (2003): https://hbr.org/2003/03/what-becomes-an-icon-most
39. As argued in this *HBR* piece: James C. Shroer, Ad spending: Growing Market Share. *Harvard Business Review* (1990). https://hbr.org/1990/01/ad -spending-growing-market-share
40. Andrew Ehrenberg, Neil Barnard, Rachel Kennedy and Helen Bloom, Advertising as creative publicity. *Journal of Advertising Research*, 42(4) (2002) 7–18. Full copy available at: https://www.researchgate.net/ publication/260555133_Brand_Advertising_As_Creative_Publicity
41. Outlined in this piece in *Campaign* magazine – https://www.campaignlive .co.uk/article/challenge-byron-sharp-grow-brand/1419995 – and in more detail in his book *How Brands Grow – What Marketers Don't Know* (2010), Oxford University Press.
42. Gérard Genette, *Paratexts: Thresholds of Interpretation*, trans. Jane. E. Lewin (1997), University of Cambridge Press.
43. See Stephanie Feiereisen, Dina Rasolofoarison, Crystal Russell and Hope Jensen Schau, One brand, many trajectories: Narrative navigation in trans-media. *Journal of Consumer Research*, 48(4) (2020) 651–681. DOI: 10.1093/jcr/ucaa046.
44. http://epapers.bham.ac.uk/2962/1/Hall,_1973,_Encoding_and_Decoding _in_the_Television_Discourse.pdf
45. Ubiquitous in marketing and advertising textbooks, the transmission (orig-inally derived from a model of electrical circuits) model of mass communi-

cation posits a source, encoding process, message, decoding and receiver in a linear sequence that emphasises one, univocal and explicit message.

46. Barbara B. Stern, A revised communication model for advertising: Multiple dimensions of the source, the message, and the recipient. *Journal of Advertising*, 23(2) (1994) 5–15. DOI: 10.1080/00913367.1994.10673438.

47. Sidney J. Levy, Symbols for sale. *Harvard Business Review*, (July–August 1959) 117–124.

48. See https://www.newswise.com/articles/foundation-reports-on-business-schools-damaging

49. Grant McCracken, Culture and consumption: A theoretical account of the structure and movement of the cultural meaning of consumer goods. *Journal of Consumer Research*, 13(1) (1986) 71–84. DOI: 10.1086/209048.

50. Russell W. Belk, Possessions and the extended self. *Journal of Consumer Research*, 15(2) (1988) 139–168. DOI: 10.1086/209154.

51. David Glen Mick and Claus Buhl, A meaning-based model of advertising experiences. *Journal of Consumer Research*, 19(3) (1992) 317–338. DOI: 10.1086/209305.

52. John W. Schouten and James H. Alexander, Subcultures of consumption: An ethnography of the new bikers. *Journal of Consumer Research*, 22(1) (1995) 43–61.

53. Eric Arnould and Craig Thompson later (2005) recorded the trajectory of qualitative, critical and socio-cultural work in consumer research in Eric J. Arnould and Craig J. Thompson, Consumer Culture Theory (CCT): Twenty years of research. *Journal of Consumer Research*, 31(4) (2005) 868–882. DOI: 10.1086/426626.

5. How does advertising 'work'?

INTRODUCTION

In Chapter 5 we revisit some common assumptions about the motives and effectiveness of advertisements. We do so in order to underline why we believe that paratextual advertising is far from an abstract theorisation, but also offers a managerial agenda for brand communication. Ask most people about what advertising is for, and they'll say it's for selling stuff. They wouldn't be wrong. But in Chapter 4 we touched on some competing theories of branding that have rather different assumptions about how advertisements do this. Holt's cultural branding approach, for example, would seem on the face of it to cohere more closely with Ehrenberg's theory that advertising works as a form of publicity, creating presence and salience for the brand, with sales resulting as a necessary consequence. The implication would seem to be that advertising should reach a wide audience, be entertaining, and sometimes be controversial, in order to spark conversations and debate.

Riess and Trout's 'mindshare' model, on the other hand, suggests that advertising that is targeted at segmented consumers to reinforce a set of distinctive brand attributes can occupy the memory of the consumer and results in increased sales. Under this scheme, linking the brand too strongly with wider cultural events or practices could be a distraction and a risk. In contrast to both of these implied positions on advertising effects, marketing and advertising textbooks usually play up the idea that an advertisement acts like a mediated salesperson, persuading the viewer to change their attitude and behaviour towards the advertised brand, and consequently buy it. In this chapter we examine some of the assumptions behind theories of advertising effect and consider them in the light of paratextual and other literary theories of advertising as text.

HOW ADVERTISING WORKS – OR DOESN'T

In spite of the hyperbolic claims often made for advertising, especially that carried on digital media, it is important to reiterate the familiar point that no one has ever proved that advertising, of any kind, can persuade someone to buy something, without other possible intervening variables claiming some credit for the purchase. Advertising's effect on sales is assumed to be obvious, but in spite of more than 100 years of research, there is still no definitive science of advertising effect that can make a causal connection between the exposure to an ad, and the purchase.[1]

There are some popular hoaxes about subliminal advertising having such an effect; for example the one perpetrated by market researcher James Vicary in 1957 who claimed that advertising messages such as 'Hungry? Eat popcorn' and 'Drink Coca-Cola' flashed within a movie at frame speeds too rapid to fall within conscious awareness greatly increased audience Coke and popcorn sales during the next interval in the show. The idea was tested by others and found ineffective, and Vicary eventually admitted that he had invented his data,[2] but in spite of no corroborating evidence, myths about advertising's 'subliminal' effects persist. The idea that an advertisement can cause a viewer to buy what is advertised has also persisted since John E. Kennedy's influential analogy that advertising is 'salesmanship in print' (referenced elsewhere in this book). Business school advertising research has, then, been motivated by the question of how advertising 'works'.[3] The assumption behind studies that put the question in this way is that questions about advertising's sales effect can be posed in a common-sense way in order to provide a definitive answer. Beneath the assumption implied in posing the question in this way is another – that advertising is one thing, and it always has one purpose, which is to persuade the viewer of the ad to buy what is being advertised very soon after viewing the ad and as a direct result of having seen it.

There are countless problems with this way of conceiving advertising effect, some of which we have touched on previously in the book. Good articles which investigate this question, such as the one by Demetrios Vakratas and Tim Ambler in note 3, do acknowledge it. Naturally, advertising is intended to sell stuff, and indeed it does, but trying to establish a line of causation between the ad exposure and the purchase gets very difficult very quickly. No doubt we have all seen ads that made us want something, or that reminded us of something we needed to get, and we got it fairly soon afterwards. If it was a social media or search ad, we might have bought the thing almost immediately, online, by clicking the buy button. Or we've seen an ad that pointed out some shortcomings of the brand we use and made us think we ought to try a new brand next time. It is, as it were, common sense that these instances do indeed sometimes occur. But even the occurrence of a sale that quickly follows the viewing of an ad cannot entirely be attributed to the ad, since, for example, we might also have been influenced by seeing other people buy and own that thing before we saw the ad, we might have been influenced by a recommendation or a review and we saw the ad soon afterwards, or there might a problem in our lives (we needed a new car tyre or washing machine) that prompted the purchase, and seeing the ad was incidental. This happens frequently with search and social advertising that is activated by a search for, say local car tyre retailers, and we are then sent dozens of similar ads. If we buy a tyre in the next week, did these ads 'work'? The answer is that they made us aware of local offers and providers, but they didn't sell anything that we weren't going to buy anyway.[4] Finally, as Morris Holbrook and Elizabeth Hirschman pointed out in their seminal consumer research article, we also often buy stuff for fun, to lift our mood, or to indulge some fantasy of our social identity.[5] This being so, of the countless ads we see that make buying stuff seem fun and status-enhancing, it is a bit of a lottery as to which ones coincide with our purchases.

We also see countless other ads to which we do not react, and we might not even notice, hence the well-known statistic we have referred to earlier in the book – the average click-through rate (CTR) for social media display ads across all platforms is under 1%[6] (the average CTR for search ads is a little higher, while there is a lot of variation between platforms and sectors). Bear in mind, also, that a click-through is just another stage in the digital 'sales funnel' (to use a very well-worn ad industry metaphor for the process of finding and organising sales prospects)[7] and it is still a long way down to the sale at the pointy end of the funnel spout. The proportion of users who click through and then ultimately buy an item is called the conversion rate, and you can imagine that at this stage of the process you're looking at something like 1% of the 1% who saw the ad and clicked on it. To be fair to digital advertising, one could imagine a similar success rate for ads on traditional media but with far less feedback about effectiveness and targeting, and at much greater cost. The reality for advertisers is that cost per person reached with advertising is far lower with search and social advertising than with traditional mass media advertising, so the economics of the process mean that both small, local providers and also global, big budget brands can do very well with search and social ads in spite of the tiny CTRs and conversion rates.

This is not to imply that the advertising environment is a formless cascade of ads that descend upon a mêlée of viewers, with the statistically inevitable result that sometimes a viewer buys something that was promoted in an ad to which the viewer was recently exposed. The relationship between advertising and sales is probably not entirely one of chance. For 200 years or more, marketers and advertisers have been astute at reducing the rate of ad redundancy through the artful timing, audience selection and design of advertisements. To take a simple example, beachwear is advertised when people are planning summer holidays. It is also often available near beaches. If it is expensive high-fashion beachwear, then it is advertised to people with higher-than-average incomes through selective media planning.[8] Nonetheless, in spite of the greatly increased precision of consumer surveillance enabled by digital media, John Wannamaker's famous aphorism about half of the money spent on advertising being wasted is probably no less true of digital ads than it is of traditional media advertising. The advantage of digital advertising is that advertisers can vary their targeting and copy in real time and watch the ROI (return on investment) react, so there is far more control and budgetary discipline than with the traditional model of creative advertising. Having said that, traditional media have made strides in their effectiveness measurement, helped of course by digital technology.

Further clouding the common-sense question of how advertising 'works' is the fact that a lot of advertising is made that was never intended to sell stuff, at least, not immediately.[9] For example, there is lots of advertising designed for audiences other than customers, such as ads designed to reassure stockholders, to engage and motivate employees and supply chain associates, ads aimed at industry regulators or politicians involved in regulatory policy, or ads designed as PR (Public Relations) to influence the business press (and through them, to influence all the above).

Advertising strategy, the ostensible purpose of the ad, can be quite specific. For example, a campaign might be motivated by a need to defend a brand from own-brand rivals, as was the case for Heinz Baked Beans which found in 1967 that their rather generic product of tinned beans in watery tomato sauce was copied by many of the supermarkets that sold it, eking away at the brand's sales. Up stepped Maurice Drake, creative at Young and Rubican, who coined one of the most famous and enduring slogans in British advertising – Beanz Meanz Heinz.[10] The annoyingly alliterative aphorism spawned dozens of connected TV spots, jingles and rhymes, and cemented the brand as market leader. Ultimately, branding, and advertising, is designed to reduce price elasticity of demand so that a brand can act as a quasi-monopoly, charging higher margins because more consumers will buy that brand unreflexively, simply putting it in the shopping basket because of the reassurance offered by the familiarity. Drake's idea sold an awful lot of Britain's staple food because it made the brand impossible to forget.

Some advertising is created simply to match the adspend of a direct competitor. If brand x has increased its ad budget for the year by 3%, so main competitor brand y does the same because if it doesn't, it'll lose market share and/or lose the confidence of investors or consumers. In such a case, of course, the precise creative content of the ad is less important than the fact that the ad is made, seen, and seen to be made and seen. Other ads are made because it has become expected over time that they will be, for example UK Christmas retail ads, or American Superbowl ads. These ads are created each year at great expense in order to feature as part of one of the major TV events of the year. If they're good, they will become talked about, shared on social media, and viewed on video sharing platforms for years to come. The broad aim of these ads is brand building, with an element of competitive paranoia (if rival A bets the house on an epic Christmas TV ad, then there is pressure from management, shareholders and analysts, and maybe consumers, for rival B to do the same).

Finally, there is also a lot of advertising made without a very clear or coherent idea of what it is intended to accomplish. Advertising strategy is very difficult to get right – it takes time, thought and resources, and there are numerous pressures to distil the advertising development process into a few days instead of a few weeks, which often results in strategy being fudged.[11] It is very easy to make bad ads, and digital media are making it much easier. Whatever the motive or the quality of execution, all the above ads do one thing, provided they are seen – they create cultural and psychological space for the brand being advertised (what Byron Sharp calls 'mental availability', as we mentioned earlier) and that in itself can create a sales momentum.

Advertising works because a lot of people need and want to buy a lot of stuff, and generally speaking the stuff that gets bought more gets advertised more, because we usually make purchasing choices from two to five alternatives, depending on the circumstances, such is the limitation of human working memory and patience. We buy the stuff we can remember, when we remember to buy it, we buy when it is convenient to us, and we buy when we need stuff. Creative advertising can generate a platform of topicality and relevance for a brand, and digital advertising can activate purchasing. We return to the idea of an advertising continuum from publicity to activation in Chapter 7.

CREATIVITY AND DIGITAL ADVERTISING

We want to briefly touch on the argument that digital advertising has made advertising creativity irrelevant. It seems intuitive that, notwithstanding all our caveats about how ads work or don't, ads that are designed cleverly will be more effective than ads that are not, all other things being equal. In this book we use the terms creativity and creative execution as labels for ad design, content, the way the ad looks, sounds, smells, feels. This is usually the distinctive human element of advertising, although a lot of the advertising content on social media and in search results is designed (or at least, tweaked) by an AI machine from a very simple template of headline, image, slogan and 'call to action' button. When the key is to get an ad in front of someone at a time when they are already almost persuaded to buy that thing, it doesn't matter too much what the ad looks like as long as it isn't so bad that it ruins the sale. AI machines are really good at using real-time AB testing to tweak the image or the headline of a social media ad until the engagement, dwell[12] or CTR numbers edge upwards. So, our friendly search and social AI machines deserve a big gold pencil for that.

There is a lot of search and social advertising. Around half of annual global adspend (all the money spent on advertising) went on the broad category of digital ads just before COVID-19 struck in 2020, and that proportion is on an upward trend.[13] Nevertheless, there is still plenty of life in creative advertising, both the kind that is executed on digital media such as video, podcast ads or social media display ads, and the kind that starts out on bought traditional media and graduates to digital as a secondary exposure or if it gets shared. There is plenty of scope for creativity in digital advertising – digital is a very large category, and includes some standout video content, the odd yet compelling ephemeral video advertising that will disappear if the viewer doesn't swipe up before the ad ends, and audio ads that are embedded within podcasts and held to the same production standards. Creativity can be applied to any genre of advertising, and there is plenty of evidence for its efficacy that flies in the face of the argument that digital has made advertising creativity redundant. It seems intuitive that the CTRs (and dwell times) for digital display and search ads might well improve if the ads were better, so that people actually watched them for pleasure or interest. On current projections the proportion of global adspend on traditional media will still be around a hefty 50% in spite of the rapid growth in digital. This, and the redundancy rate in digital advertising, means there is still a compelling case for advertising that is actually well conceived in its strategy and creative. In other words, good advertising is better than bad advertising, whatever the medium. It is easy to imagine that making an ad as compelling as a good story is a great way to get viewers on board, so they pay attention to the ad, spend some time watching it, and maybe talk about it, share it on social media, and even like the brand as a result of enjoying the ad. We all like to be entertained, diverted, intrigued, and advertising as a concept is ineffably dreary. Advertising that is worth watching is much better in every way than advertising that is endured.

PARATEXTUAL ADVERTISING EFFECTS

Advertising, then, is not one thing: it is many things, and it can do many things, most but not all of which are broadly aimed at shifting stock, stimulating sales and ramping up revenue, along with a multitude of aims that in some way facilitate all the above, including reassuring stock markets, regulators, policymakers and employees, as well as playing poker with competitive rivals by committing sums to the advertising budget that said rivals do not want to match. There is no conceivable need of or use for a grand theory of advertising effects, even if one were possible. We acknowledge, though, that seeing advertisements as paratexts that inflect the meaning of the brand coheres broadly with brand building advertising and the Ehrenberg[14] inspired idea that consumer advertising mostly generates publicity for a brand, leading to increased market share and generating sales in the long term. Advertising creates a cultural and psychological space for a brand, and it does this best by being interesting, fun and persistent. Sales, attention, engagement, affective responses, votes, donations, whatever the ultimate aim of the advertising, tend to follow when advertisements that people like are seen by a lot of people.

A focus on advertisements as paratexts highlights the lines of connection that suddenly become visible when signs and symbols align. Admittedly, this is not very likely when we see local digital ads for locally provided products and services traders, but it is far more likely when an ad for a familiar brand pops into our social media browsing. Many brands do pay attention to occupying the whole media bandwidth with their advertising strategy, from TV spots to sponsored Facebook posts, precisely in order to generate these lines of intertextual connection. It is easy to see the value in this, both as a source of reinforcement and recognition, as a means of extending the audience reach of a TV spot by offering micro versions of the ad on social media to audiences who don't watch TV, or as an activation device designed to turn the wide visibility and positive reception of a popular TV spot into hard sales and hard cash. The sales funnel[15] and its digital adaptations neatly illustrate this principle. The big creative ads, those of the brand building ilk, can be good at corralling wide audiences into the rim of the funnel, while more sales-oriented advertising (for example, your cheap digital ads with their 'call to action' links) are better at clinching the sale at the business end of the funnel. Brand recognition can be a powerful motivator at any stage in the 'customer journey' (or CX) and the concept of the paratext can help us to see how a fragmented brand presence in the advertising landscape is seen holistically by consumers.

It is implied in conceiving advertisements as texts that the content of an ad consists in meaning. The reader must make sense of the content, and to do so there must be some implicit or explicit reference to other texts beyond the ad. In practical terms, the reader might have seen some other paratext that informed the way that they construed the ad, such as, say, reviews of the commodity or the brand, comments from friends, news stories, and so forth. There might also be situational factors that influence the reader's response to the ad, such as their ad literacy and knowledge of intertextual references in the ad, and also their financial situation, emotional mood and temperament at the time they see the ad. All of these variables mean that the ad cannot be isolated as the sole motivating force behind the consumer's response. The upshot of this is that the holy grail of advertising – the search for an ideal combination of copy, image and creative (sound, colour) that pushes our red button to make us buy – is a chimera.

Advertising texts have the capacity to captivate, charm, amuse, frighten, fascinate, appal, nauseate, excite: indeed, they have the properties of texts. But, self-evidently, they do not have the capacity to respond to our objections to purchase in real time the way that a sales professional would try to do in a face-to-face encounter.[16] Ads do not have skills of real-time persuasive argumentation, at least not yet – the development of AI chatbots will no doubt move some way towards this in the future, but, like a bad salesperson, they might have trouble deviating from their script. In any event, for the time being, advertisements, even assisted by AI chatbots, do not possess the rhetorical skills, charm and intuitive gifts to sell in the way that a personal selling professional can. As mediated communications they have their own qualities and potentialities, and we feel that conceiving advertisements as texts captures some of these qualities.

THE PARATEXTUAL LOGIC OF IMPLICIT ADVERTISING

We say more about implicit advertising in the subsequent chapters. For the present, we want to touch on the increase in implicit advertising – that is, advertising that does not have an explicit sales orientation – because we see paratextual theory as a useful means of theorising the shift in the creative logic of advertising, from the explicit, to the implicit. The rapid growth over the last 20 years of sponsorship, brand content, product placement and other implicit forms of promotional communication bears testimony to this shift. Sponsorship, for example, has evolved from a clunky association with a sport, literary event, charity or other worthy (and publicity worthy) event to a many-headed Hydra of hybrid advertising forms that combine elements of brand placement, content, celebrity endorsement, UGC (User Generated Content), PR, buzz and activation. Red Bull and GoPro, for example, have taken sponsorship to multi-platform executions that defy the old promotional mix categories. GoPro users can film their adventure sports activities and upload them to a website maintained and curated by the brand. This is user-generated creative advertising that comes with guaranteed authenticity and represents great value for the brand. Red Bull has generated a global presence by associating the brand with many sports and adrenalin events, from cliff diving to white water rafting. These sponsored activities become advertisements through the many action clips uploaded to video sharing platforms. Sponsorship was once about showing the logo, just as product placement was about 'showing the can'. Today, the seamless connective web of internet platforms means that, for example, sponsorship of a football team can mean individual playing stars sporting the brand in TV interviews, a visible presence on the team shirts, around the perimeter of the playing pitch, and on the pitch itself during televised matches and in eternally repeated video match highlights, a visible presence on a back-screen in every club announcement and on every fan broadcast, and, often, extensions into local schools or sports team sponsorship.

The execution of techniques like sponsorship and product placement usually (although not always) leaves the viewer/user/reader to make the link between brand and context. The advertising motive of the content is implicit. There is no need to labour the association with clunky announcements of the 'this event is brought to you by' type. Media users know this already, the association acts as a silent intertext, and the fact is rhetorically more powerful if it is not laboured. The world of commerce now seems to have a greater understanding of the ideological force of implicit advertising as a device that renders normal and everyday associations that would seem incongruous were they made explicit. It is easy to imagine the hard commercial benefits of, say, Red Bull sponsoring cliff diving, since the predominantly young, driven and athletic audience would be the most likely audience to consume the energy drink. The sponsorship doubles as advertising through the social sharing of such events. The aggregate effect is powerfully paratextual, sprinkling texts through the off- and online worlds of relevant audiences to inflect the meaning of the brand.

We see paratextual advertising, then, as a theoretically informed perspective, not a category, of advertising. It reflects a way advertising and its effects can be better understood, it does not describe a set of advertising forms, media, types or genres. It embraces the idea that advertising can sell stuff, not in a direct way analogous to a personal selling encounter, but in an indirect way by investing brands, commodities and consumption practices with allure, mystique and with many kinds of appeal, such as appeals to status, to fear of social opprobrium, to self-image, and so on. We also see paratextuality as a particularly useful approach to theorising advertisements that seem to eschew all the hackneyed genre conventions of advertising and, instead, simply give a presence to a brand in a setting that confers ideological legitimacy and cultural familiarity on the brand.

The shift in the strategic logic of creative advertising from the explicit sales appeal to the implicit brand presence also reflects changes in media production and consumption. Edward Bernays, Sigmund Freud's nephew and wartime propagandist turned PR expert,[17] felt that communication that was designed to manipulate attitudes and behaviour was most effective when it was anointed with the authority of an official source. He therefore contrived to create events that featured in news or entertainment media, or crafted announcements and reports that came framed as authoritative and objective information from spuriously official-sounding committees. Today, in the UK, the news coverage and source credibility given to countless mysteriously funded 'think tanks' and 'research groups' bear witness to the way Bernays' ideas have been adopted by modern political propagandists (as they were by Joseph Goebbels for the Third Reich, to the Jewish Bernays' discomfort). Paratextual theory hints at the way in which ideas and images that appear epitextual – that is, outwith the bounds of the primary text – can powerfully frame the way that the primary text is understood, whether that primary text is a political party, an ideology or a consumer brand. There is no neat dichotomy between ads that sell and ads that publicise – both, clearly, do both. Branded content is popular, for example, because it builds brand presence and helps to drive audiences to the brand website. BMW have produced their free-to-access, expensively produced action movies[18] for more than a decade because they know the movies increase traffic into BMW showrooms as well as helping the brand's prestige and global audience reach.

CONCLUDING COMMENTS

In Chapter 5 we have taken a superficial but broad view of some of the most prominent managerial theories of how advertising 'works', that is, how it sells stuff, in order to locate our paratextual approach. In keeping with most other literary theories of advertising, we do not focus on the persuasive selling potential of a single advertisement. Self-evidently, the well-known theories of advertising communication and persuasion (AIDA: the transmission communication model[19]) conceive of advertisements as mediated salespeople, and although AI systems are deepening the interactional potential of advertising with chatbots, advertisements have not yet acquired the ability to respond spontaneously to objections to purchase in the same way as a personal sales professional.

In Chapter 6 we turn away from naïve models of how advertising 'works' to ideas of advertisements as vehicles for telling stories. This way of understanding advertising, on the face of it, aligns with paratextual and other literary theories of advertising, although, as we shall see, there are problems with the application of theories of storytelling and narrative to advertising.

NOTES

1. Some academics will be keen to argue this point but there isn't: trust us, we're marketing academics.

2.   See this excellent 2017 piece by Marsha Appel, Of sex and ice cubes: The great subliminal advertising scare. https://www.warc.com/newsandopinion/opinion/of-sex-and-ice-cubes-the-great-subliminal-advertising-scare/2558

3.   For example, Demetrios Vakratsas and Tim Ambler, How advertising works: What do we really know? *Journal of Marketing*, 63(1) (1999) 26–43. DOI: 10.2307/1251999.

4.   'Retargeting' algorithms are not very good at stopping ads being targeted at us once we have bought the advertised thing.

5.   Morris B. Holbrook and Elizabeth C. Hirschman, The experiential aspects of consumption: Consumer fantasies, feelings, and fun. *Journal of Consumer Research*, 9(2) (1982), 132–140. DOI: 10.1086/208906.

6.   This is one source on CTRs of many: https://www.acquisio.com/blog/agency/what-is-a-good-click-through-rate-ctr/

7.   We discuss this and other (both well-worn and not so worn) industry metaphors, theories and panaceas in the 2021 5th edition of our text, *Advertising and Promotion*, published by Sage (and since this is a book about advertising by advertising academics, here is a click-through opportunity to purchase the book: https://us.sagepub.com/en-us/nam/advertising-and-promotion/book271888).

8.   Find a 2021 discussion of some of the pitfalls and benefits of digital advertising here: https://www.linkedin.com/pulse/digital-advertising-doesnt-work-sascha-st%C3%BCrze; and see another one here: https://hbr.org/2021/02/what-digital-advertising-gets-wrong

9.   The UK advertising trade body, the IPA, stocks a lot of case studies showing the many different ways in which ad effectiveness can be measured for many different strategic purposes: https://ipa.co.uk/initiatives/effectiveness

10.   See https://www.creativereview.co.uk/beanz-meanz-heinz-slogan/

11.   We discuss the process of developing advertising strategy and creative in our book: Chris Hackley and Rungpaka Amy Hackley, *Advertising and Promotion*, 5th Edition (2021), Sage (https://us.sagepub.com/en-us/nam/advertising-and-promotion/book271888), and also in Chapter 7 of this book.

12.   Dwell time is how long a user spends looking at an ad. CTR (click-through rate) is the number of those users who click on the ad for more information, usually ending up at the brand website landing page.

13.   Here is a 2021 projection of growth in digital adspend as a whole: https://www.statista.com/statistics/237974/online-advertising-spending-worldwide/. The proportion that digital ad spend is of the total global ad spend is projected to rise from roughly 50% in 2019 to more than 60% in 2024: https://www.emarketer.com/content/global-digital-ad-spending-update-q2-2020

14.   The definitive Ehrenberg et al. paper in advertising as publicity is discussed by Byron Sharp here: https://www.marketingscience.info/wp-content/uploads/2021/10/Ehrenbergs-Views-on-Advertising.pdf

15.   There are countless expositions of the digital sales funnel, here is one: https://www.bluecorona.com/blog/new-digital-marketing-funnel-strategies/

16.   The standard personal selling formula is to 'answer the objections' to purchase that a sales 'prospect' (i.e. a prospective customer) raises. This

often entails learning a 'patter' that anticipates all the likely 'objections' to buying. As one might expect, in practice this rhetorical technique turns out to be not so much a Socratic dialogue as a sophistical one. This can descend to outright bullying and intimidation with 'high-pressure' techniques, as with reports of timeshare operators who invite prospects to a presentation with a free gift and promising 'no commitment required' only to have bouncers blocking exit from the building until a contract for a timeshare apartment has been signed.

17. See this well-written introduction to Bernays' ideas: https://theconversation .com/the-manipulation-of-the-american-mind-edward-bernays-and-the -birth-of-public-relations-44393

18. Listed here: https://www.imdb.com/search/title/?companies=co0004108

19. These theories are reviewed in Chris Hackley, Theorizing advertising: Managerial, scientific and cultural approaches, chapter 6 in Pauline MacLaran, Michael Saren, Barbara Stern and Mark Tadajewski (Eds) *The Sage Handbook of Marketing Theory* (2010), Sage, pp. 89–107; and also outlined in Chris Hackley and Rungpaka Amy Hackley, *Advertising and Promotion*, 5th Edition (2021), Sage.

6. Storytelling and paratextual advertising

INTRODUCTION

In Chapter 6 we turn away from the naïve behavioural theories of how advertising persuades that we discussed in Chapter 5, to consider the possibilities of advertising texts as narrative devices of entertainment. Of course, persuasion and entertainment are by no means mutually exclusive, as we discuss later in this chapter. But, if an advertisement cannot be a salesperson, as we maintain, can it really be a story? And if so, how does telling a story fit with advertising's aim of selling stuff? We can all think of long-form TV spots that tell fully elaborated stories. For example, the 2013 three-minute tearjerker, from Thai mobile phone provider True Move H,[1] has garnered more than 40 million views on YouTube, while another example from Thailand, a 2015 epic of no less than five minutes (selling CCTV systems), has registered more than 100 million views.[2] But, such cinematic extravagance aside, the majority of advertisements are not like this: they are short, incomplete, distilled with almost subliminal brevity. Is storytelling, then, about a sub-genre of advertising, and not about most of it? Or, if all advertising has story elements, how can we make sense of this?

In this chapter we explore these questions to move towards our conclusion, which is that ideas about storytelling, brands and advertising can only make sense within a paratextual framework. This is because neither the advertisement nor the brand can be a story. The advertisement is a paratext, a margin note, a footnote or a cover blurb to the real story. The real story is about the brand, and this is a notional story, a perpetually unwritten story, elaborated only by the paratexts that surround it and connect to it, which both inscribe and erase the brand story. These are some of the complexities of brand storytelling and advertising that we will explore in Chapter 6, drawing on theories of narrative transportation, storytelling and narrative analysis.

THE PROBLEMATIC IDEA OF STORYTELLING IN ADVERTISING

Conceiving of the advertisement as a text rather than a bundle of data, and the consumer of advertising as a reader rather than as a data processing machine, begs the question of what, exactly, is being read, and how is it being read? We have alluded to creative advertising that evokes reader responses of heightened affect, heightened recall, engagement or absorption, all of which are the kinds of response one might expect from a reader who is absorbed in a narrative. Storytelling is not only a universal human activity, but a psychological organising principle through which we make sense of our world. Our paratextual perspective on advertising draws on ideas from the literary field so it seems inevitable that the idea of a story will be pertinent to what we want to say. The problem is that stories tend to have distinct narrative elements such as scene setting, characterisation, protagonist, problem/dilemma, journey/narrative arc, and resolution, while paratexts are usually highly distilled stories, if they can be identified as stories at all, as opposed to merely semiotic intertexts.

Many advertisements clearly try to transport the reader to another world, a more vivid, satisfying and happy world than the one they currently occupy – but only so that you buy something when you get there. Are marketing types waxing about the brand 'story' not indulging in a bit of delusion or hyperbole? Is it flattering advertisements to call them 'stories'? What is more, if great works of literature have enormous textual gaps into which the reader can project interpretations, as Wolfgang Iser suggested with reader-response theory, can we really apply principles of storytelling to ads that are usually more suggestive gap than explicit narrative? Is it still a story if the reader is also the author?

Part of the fascination of advertisements is the way that, done well, some ads can distil a story into a form so condensed that there seems to be no traditional narrative as such, yet the story somehow unfolds in an emotionally compelling way, with the viewer as omniscient narrator. The cinematographic, musical, typographic, poetic and other craft skills involved in such ads, not to mention the psychological insight, are impressive when one unpicks the ad in detail, even if the idea of the ad might have been based on an intuition. Yet, does it make sense to speak of advertisements as stories, in the sense that they reveal a point of view on events that lead from an initial state to an outcome or different state, with scene setting, protagonist, plot and so forth, since they rarely conform to typical narrative structures? Storytelling devices such as Aristotle's unities, the story arc from challenge through adversity to redemption, or even Joseph Campbell's monomyth and the hero's journey that we mention below, are seldom parts of advertising training or education. Or, are advertisements some other form of narrative unit that suggestively deploys elements of stories without the connecting fibre that would normally hold the elements of a story together?

Later in the chapter we discuss the possibility of a continuum from fully articulated story advertising paratexts to brand intertexts that spark associative meaning and are open to conscious or unconscious semiotic readings, in an endless spiral of brand texts appearing within other brand texts. This line of discussion moves towards an implied poetics of digital intertextuality – to what extent might fragmented brand appearances spark associations that provoke reader-like audience responses of engagement and emotion? And, if brand advertising is becoming a whirl of branded content within other branded content within more branded content, and the consumer/reader is allowed more and more interpretive licence, how might brand management and/or consumers/readers try to impose order on this intertextual chaos? And should they even try?

Certainly, some peritextual examples of Gérard Genette's notion of the paratext would hardly qualify as storytelling vehicles, any more than a sight of the preface or cover blurb could give an account of the novel to which they refer. Like literary texts, brands have technical peritextual additions to the main text, such as lists of ingredients on food packaging or lists of side effects on medicines. These peritextual paratexts are significant in that they help construct the brand as a legitimate product that is systematically known, tested and officially approved, but their storytelling capacity is obviously limited. However, brand paratextuality also embraces textual devices more fertile in their narrative potential than mere lists of ingredients. Even Genette would agree that certain epitexts around literary works could indeed qualify as mini storytelling vehicles. Published reviews, parodies, serialisations, poster advertisements, dramatisations and interviews with the author might all have story elements. They also all possess rich potential for inflecting the narrative direction the reader will take through the primary text. Indeed, brand paratexts such as advertisements, memes, UGC (User Generated Content), reviews and the like have a paratextual relation not only to the brand, but to each other. The intense narrative distillation we sometimes see in a well-drafted advertisement can be cast into a hall of mirrors to show us many variations on the theme that change, depending on our own position.

But, again, is this really about stories in the sense of having a setting, a hero, a problem, a resolution, or is it merely a kinetic kind of intertextuality in which a central element of the traditional story, the narrative arc, is left open to the instinct of readers to complete in their own way? If that is the case, should this kind of paratextual elicitation qualify as storytelling at all? In an account of advertising storytelling should we try to nuance the distinction between ads that tell stories, ads that cue certain story-like readings, and ads that spark intertextual associations that may have story elements or may be part of consumers' life stories but fall short of being storytelling ads? After all, we know from previous research that some types of advertisements can evoke narrative transportation, the feeling of being transported imaginatively to another world, but not all ads do this, because not all need to do this – it all depends on what the ad strategy might be.[3]

CHARACTERISTICS OF STORIES IN ADVERTISING

The power of stories to invest advertising with emotional resonance and, as a result, increase attention, engagement and recall of the brand is often subject to hyperbole in the marketing industry. Self-evidently, brands tell stories about themselves, just as advertising tells us stories about ourselves and the ways we live. Victorian entrepreneur and branding visionary Thomas Holloway's patented medicines were often advertised with vivid (and no doubt apocryphal) testimonials of the wonderful effects of the ointment. His advertising copy for ointment was ahead of its time:

> 'It may be rubbed into the system so as to reach any internal complaint: it even penetrates the bones as salt does meat: by these means it cures the most hidden wounds, such as sores or ulcers in the throat, stomach, liver, abdomen, spine or other parts. It is an infallible remedy...'[4]

Needless to say, there were no advertising regulators checking the veracity of product claims in Holloway's day.

The tin of one of Holloway's ointments featured an injured American Civil War soldier being assisted to the field hospital by two colleagues, lending specious visual evidence to the claims that the product can cure almost any injury. Holloway, the founder of the college later honoured with Queen Victoria's endorsement as Royal Holloway,[5] knew how to spin an engaging yarn. His instinct for interesting paratexts was such that he also paid playwrights to insert the brand names of his medicines into London stage plays of the time. The archetypal circus impresario P.T. Barnum was another marketing genius who, like Holloway, remains unmentioned in marketing management textbooks and uncelebrated in the top university business schools,[6] yet his instincts for PR (Public Relations) and storytelling were exemplary.[7]

The treatment of storytelling in industry blogs and feature pieces tends to lean towards the polemical, as if marketers who grasp that their art is about telling stories have discovered a radical new insight. It seems simply intuitive that advertising tells stories, not *War and Peace* or *Gone With the Wind* or even *The Old Man and the Sea* types of stories, but much simpler story forms, perhaps more akin to folk tales or nursery rhymes (and countless ads use nursery rhymes as their template[8]). For example, many ad campaigns on UK TV have dramatised vignettes of family life that portray the brand as a sort of material artefact, enabling social relations and deepening family bonds. The Oxo brand of gravy mix was portrayed as an essential accessory to domestic bliss in no less than 42 episodes[9] of the Oxo Family in the 1980s,[10] (revived with new characters in 2016[11]). Renault's Papa and Nicole ads of the 1990s showed uptight British families how indulgent French fathers dealt with their daughters' illicit romantic liaisons (by ignoring them, apparently). The Gold Blend ads captivated the UK with a romance that began with a borrowed jar of instant coffee.[12] These examples may have been TV spots from an era in which half the UK population watched terrestrial TV in real time, but they are striking examples of storied advertising. More recent examples tend to be cross-platform in their execution, such as the entire storyworld created by the comparethemarket.com meerkats we discuss earlier in the book, where we have self-contained story vignettes told separately in TV spots, on their website, and in published books.

Then there are the brands that are not the subject of stories but, rather, are woven into other, bigger stories, so that, featuring as part of the scene or script in movies, TV soaps, radio podcasts, novels or other entertainments, they become part of the story (or even the hero of it, as in the BMW action movies[13]). In this way, brands, even in a minor role, can become part of the consumer's life story, embedded in a personal experience of film entertainment, even if the brand is hardly noticed at the time. Brands do not score well on unprompted recall tests when they are subtle parts of the scene of a piece of film entertainment. However, the short-term recall tests beloved of marketers only measure semantic memory, also called explicit memory, that is the immediate recall of facts. Such prompted or unprompted recall tests do not take into account the power of episodic or implicit memory, those types of memory that are unconscious but can be triggered by experiences.

For example, in one piece of the authors' research, a participant told how they only recalled a scene in a TV soap set in a Dairy Queen ice cream store when they walked past one of the stores in the street.[14] The sight of, say, a 7-Eleven store in a street scene of a *Superman* movie[15] does not in itself carry any element of persuasive force impelling the viewer to go to their nearest 7-Eleven – indeed, convenience stores just don't work like that. What such brand visibility does, though, is to leverage and reinforce the brand as a familiar feature in the consumer's experiential landscape. That, ideologically normalised, presence and familiarity breaks barriers and leads to habitual consumption. In addition, such passive exposure has publicity side effects, such as media stories about the brands featuring in the latest *Superman* movie. Our point here of course reflects the benefit to brands that accrue from the publicity value of advertising, as articulated by Andrew Ehrenberg and colleagues (also mentioned previously).[16] For some advertising commentators and practitioners such as Paul Feldwick,[17] advertising should be regarded as a branch of showbusiness,[18] and the mutual endorsement of entertainment brand and advertised brand is a natural evolution of marketing.

There are also many advertisements, while not exactly stories, that connect with human stories by tapping into folklore, myth and legend through their evocative symbolism. The mythic symbolism of brands such as Nike[19] is well known – the ancient Greek goddess of victory creates modern myths of victors and victories with suggestive vignettes of triumph against odds, while the double-tailed Siren logo of Starbucks[20] has become globally famous and a source of many stories.[21] But there is nothing new about the selling power of myth. The art of bringing a myth-ical element to mundane consumption is as old as print advertising.[22] These myth-marketing ads are trying to achieve a cultural resonance by reminding us of something that has, perhaps, been lost in our collective memories, or, at least, of something that we subconsciously want to be reminded of. Many fragrance ads, for example, imply that the user will be transported into a dream world of primitive passion that evinces a time, and a lack of inhibition, long past in human history.

THE AUDIENCE AS HERO

The idea that we might pass through a threshold into a world in which we are reinvented and renewed is a powerful feature of human psychology and of dramatic art, and brands often play on this motivation by implying that they are liminal entities that can transport us into new worlds. Many advertisements from every sector can be seen to leverage the idea of personal transformation. In one research paper, we drew on anthropologist Victor Turner's ideas to suggest that liminoid advertising appeals imply that the brand itself acts as a threshold object that can transform the life, identity and experience of the user.[23] A 'New You' is, after all, a staple of advertising copywriting, not only for the sportswear,[24] diet plans[25] and cosmetic surgery[26] sectors, but also, as we show in the paper, for selling house paint, apartments and cars as well. Turner is best known for his work on rites of passage (marriage, birth and funeral rites, or modern rituals such as school graduation or ceremonies of status or initiation) that transform the participant's social identity. Turner[27] elaborated on van Gennep's[28] seminal work to argue that modern consumer societies make use of truncated versions of traditional rites of passage that are not connected to ritual process, a phenomenon Turner called existential liminality. In consumer versions of rites of passage, participation is voluntary not compulsory, and the outcome is not permanent. All that is preserved is the liminal phase, the phase in the middle of rites of passage when the participant occupies a status that is neither of their old identity, nor yet of their new one. Turner used the term liminoid to express the playful and impermanent character of this experience. Reality TV shows are perhaps a good example,[29] since participants are selected, subject to trials under the direction of a shaman (or talent show panel judge), watched by an audience, and, finally, they shed their old identity (as an anonymous member of the public) and assume their new identity as a para-celebrity or reality star. The marketing/entertainment industry seems to have developed a production line for these para-celebrities, such is their value as advertising vehicles.[30]

The idea of a liminal process is reflected in a stock resource for advertising storytelling, the hero's journey. This was powerfully expressed by Joseph Campbell, author of *The Hero with a Thousand Faces*,[31] in which he combines myth and psychoanalysis in his account of the monomyth, a universal story of human aspiration. The hero's journey from anonymity or misery through difficult adventures towards, ultimately, a heroic status, has been the inspiration for countless ads (such as Apple's HomePod, and many other examples on the *Thearetical* blog[32]). The travel and tourism industry is one of the sectors most wedded to heroic storytelling as it teases the audience with tales of exotic adventures into which they can project themselves both imaginatively and literally, such as in 2019 campaigns promoting Oregon, USA, as a tourism venue, China Airlines and Thomas Cook (the now defunct British tour operator).[33] The hero's journey seems to be particularly evident in destination brand advertising,[34] presumably because it expresses the urge of the urban dweller to seek far-away lands, challenging and life affirming experiences, perhaps a new life, and, of course, a new you. The best travel experiences also include a little deprivation and struggle, as befitting a hero's journey, but the firm friends made of fellow travellers on the way, and the vision of earthly paradise at the end, make the struggle worthwhile. The powerful emotional resonance that stories can have is in no doubt and it seems that some types of consumption lend themselves more aptly to myth-evoking treatments than others.

ADVERTISING GOES TO THE MOVIES

People generally don't seek out ads to watch, but we all enjoy entertainment. Brands benefit from being part of entertaining media content, whether that content happens to be an advertisement, a podcast, a sports event, a novel or stage play, or a movie or TV show. Some of the examples of advertisements we've noted so far tell a story in a linear way, for example by portraying someone as unhappy and unfulfilled before they buy the brand, and very happy/more attractive/more successful/more fulfilled after they've bought it. There is an art to this, and advertising is such a flexible form of textual communication that it can tell stories in ways that challenge linear readings. Telling a story well in a long-form TV ad is difficult enough, but it gets more difficult as the budget and time constraints close in. Moving the narrative along in as few frames as possible is not only necessary in advertising because of the budget on one side and because of the limited window of viewing attention on the other, but it also carries an aesthetic force, like a neatly condensed aphorism or a powerful poetic phrase. Viewers feel like participants when the story engages us, and the effect is more telling when we are led deep into a narrative by an actor's raised eyebrow, by a rapid juxtaposition of scenes, or by a well-crafted and delivered word or two of dialogue.

Given the storytelling craft skills needed for both movies and advertising, it's no accident that so many famous Hollywood movie producers and directors learned their trade sharpening their storytelling skills on the highly condensed format of the 20-second TV ad,[35] from David Puttnam (e.g. *Chariots of Fire*) and Alan Parker (e.g. *Midnight Express*) to David Fincher (e.g. *Fight Club, Mank*), Ridley Scott (*Alien*) and Michael Bay (*Transformers*). Some established movie directors now do the reverse and take commissions to make ads after having become successful in feature movies. Today, there seems to be no stigma in 'selling out' creatively to the money men. Indeed, the cultural, creative and media industries seem to have almost merged with the promotional industries, such are the common craft skills, creative values and working styles.[36]

While there is value for brands in being part of stories as features of the scene or script in movies, TV dramas and video games, media brands themselves can be useful sources of insight into paratextual branding. Chloe Preece and colleagues represented the longevity of the James Bond[37] movie franchise brand through assemblage theory, drawing on multiple archival and other sources to illustrate the brand's evolving reception over 55 years of changing socio-historical contexts. Bond has remained hugely popular over the course of more than half a century, across many cultures and many profound changes in socio-historical events and sensibilities. The Bond brand has a nebulous quality, being both vivid and rather vague, subject to continuous making and remaking through its paratextual manifestations. Bond is a useful example of the ambiguity of the brand space because this is a brand (or franchise) that has evolved from a literary form into movies, with many authors iterating the original concept. Millions of consumers around the world will recognise the name James Bond and each will have an idea of what Bond represents, and the same can be said of Coca-Cola and McDonald's, yet it is hard if not impossible to express precisely what this meaning is that seems to be shared by so many millions of people from every culture on earth.

The Bond franchise has this ambiguous quality in spades, even though there is an official Bond canon – a set of primary texts. Since the original Bond author, Ian Fleming, created the character and set out his adventures in 12 books and two collections of short stories, a number of other authors have been commissioned to write further stories since Fleming's death in 1964, some of which became movies.[38] Alongside the inevitable inconsistencies in the portrayal of Bond by different actors (the effete and ironic Bond persona of Roger Moore, for example, is the antithesis of the gritty portrayal by the first and original Bond, Sean Connery), the various book (and screenplay) authors also each had their own take on Bond. Fleming himself was hardly a stickler for consistency in the original Bond canon. Many moviegoers identify Bond with a quintessential type of Eton-educated Englishness, although the character was given Scottish antecedents by Fleming after he saw how well Scot Sean Connery performed the role in the first Bond movie, the 1963 release, *Dr. No.* Other deviations from the canon were commercially motivated. In the Fleming books, Bond always wore Rolex watches (both Fleming and Connery were fans of the brand) and Rolex was the main featured watch in the first 18 movies, with occasional walk-on parts for Seiko and TAG Heuer, but *Licence to Kill* in 1989 was the last appearance for Rolex as Omega became the official watch partner for Bond movies with the 1995 release of *Goldeneye.*[39]

In the 2006 release, *Casino Royale*, many purist Bond fans were outraged with a scene in which a lady admiringly enquired as to the brand of Bond's timepiece. 'Rolex?' 'No Omega.' In spite of the clunkiest of product placements, the movie gross did not suffer, and *Casino Royale* became the fourth highest-grossing Bond movie.[40] Two years later, in *Quantum of Solace*, Bond walked into a bar and ordered a Heineken beer, something the real Bond would have been far too much of a Martini snob to do, and the producers were so unashamed that they had the actor Daniel Craig appear in print ads drinking Heineken[41] (neatly leveraging the intertexts of actor, movie, print ad and beer). By then, in spite of the objections of some movie buffs, the distinction between entertainment brands and non-entertainment brands became blurred, and audience cynicism had given way to the expectation that brands help the verisimilitude in film entertainment.[42] Gone are the days when audiences would accept a scene prop with masking tape stuck over the brand name. Props managers and producers have to show branded items in the scene in order for it to seem realistic, and the brands themselves have to fit with the scene, the plot and the characters.

TRANSMEDIA ADVERTISING

Transmedia storytelling is more common in East Asian cinema where it originated, although it has become a buzz term in Western advertising. Relatively few Western movies engage in the transmedia practice of extending the plot and major character development through a non-movie platform, as the Wachowski brothers did when they ended the *Matrix* franchise by killing off Morpheus in a computer game.[43] *Matrix* fans were not happy with that development – they felt that the authority of the primary text of the movie trilogy had somehow been violated by the plot extension onto a computer game, which shows that brand managers should choose their paratexts carefully. From a commercial perspective, it is possible that some computer gamers encountering Morpheus in the game might have been curious to see the movies, although most players would have been led from the movies to the game.

There are striking demographic and generational differences in media consumption patterns, and advertising practice today has to follow audiences through the expanding media landscape. Stephanie Feiereisen[44] and colleagues demonstrated in their study of TV consumption that modern audiences are able to enter media (and indeed, other) brands at many different points of entry. The shrinkage of audiences for traditional media, especially TV and print, means that as a matter of commercial necessity consumer ad campaigns have to use multiple platforms to achieve the required audience reach.

Feiereisen and colleagues focused on media brands but also showed that non-media brands could benefit from transmedia executions that not only increased audience reach but allowed different trajectories of entry into the brand. As Preece and colleagues showed, a brand with reach and longevity can mean different things to different people whilst retaining some essential filament that serves to convince all the audience members that they are, somehow, engaged with the same entity. The brand paratexts circulate amongst audiences and align in moments of clarity when the meaning of the brand seems to resonate, only for the meaning to change when the moment passes and new paratexts circulate to inscribe new meanings into the ambiguous vacuum of meaning that is the brand space.[45]

Other movie paratexts, designed to be overtly promotional, seem to be more successful at widening the audience reach, such as the long-standing relationship between McDonalds and Disney whereby the new releases are promoted on the fast food packaging, complete with themed plastic toy. Of course, toys based on movie characters act as paratextual references for the movies and the Spielberg *Star Wars* franchise was probably the first to really exploit the potential of the movie as a promotional vehicle for sales of toys and action figures, and the toys and action figures as promotional vehicles for the movies.

BRAND STORIES AS PROPS IN CONSUMER LIFE STORIES

In Chapter 2 we discussed the idea of reading media texts, but we did not discuss different ways of reading, or reading practices. We can easily conceive of the difference between, say, focused reading, speed reading, skim reading, interrupted or inattentive and superficial reading. We can also conceive of readers with very different reading skills and interests, such as novice readers or expert readers, with vastly differing vocabularies and comprehension skills. When we consider electronic media content, with all its attendant elements of visual, aural, spatial and tactile elements, we can see that the idea of reading, so simple an idea to the literate, embraces a complex and varied activity. Within this complexity it seems to be universally true, nonetheless, that everyone of average intelligence has an innate grasp of the idea of a story, even if they are illiterate, such is the significance of the story (including oral traditions) as an organising principle of human psychology. It follows, then, that there is a great range of narrative forms that have a storytelling capacity, and it also seems plausible that sensible advertisers, and authors, would try to craft the stories they tell in forms that make sense to the audience they wish to activate. We can infer, then, that storytelling through paratexts is only limited by the imaginations of authors, and of consumers.

When it comes to storytelling, paratextual theory helps us to stretch the idea of storytelling across most types of ads, from long TV spots that tell a relatively elaborated story, to fragmented brand exposures that feature within other content as elements of other stories, or indeed as elements of the consumer's own life story. So, for example, a stuffed Uri, Oleg or Aleksandr meerkat toy might be understood through its location in the meerkat family storyworld created by VCCP for comparethemarket. com.[46] The momentary sight of a stuffed animal invokes past encounters with the wider storyworld and its attended paratexts, such is the power of visual memory.[47] As our experience of media becomes more intimate and pervasive, the capacity of brands and brand images to act as Madeleine objects (in Marcel Proust's story[48]) is intensified.

These brand encounters are woven into the fabric of our lives and become objects in our lived experience, linking the brand objects (and designs, jingles, names, images) with our most intimate memories.[49] Understanding advertisements as paratexts gives us a theoretically informed thread with which to connect all the various types of brand content, and it allows us to understand something of the psychology of how brand meaning is evinced by the totality of its appearances across media channels and platforms. A person who has seen the Bond movie and remembers the scene we mention above might then be served a Heineken beer in a hotel or a restaurant when having a meal with friends and be reminded momentarily of the scene and of Bond. That same person might go home on the underground train and see a poster with Daniel Craig swigging a Heineken, and they might see discarded branded cans of the beer (hopefully in waste bins) on their walk home from the train station. Such paratextual brand appearances do not tell stories in and of themselves, but through intertextuality they connect the consumer with other stories that are personal to that consumer. The visit to the movies to see *Casino Royale* might have been an enjoyable evening with a friend or lover, followed by a nice restaurant meal. This very old Dutch beer brand could also achieve other outcomes through the huge audience reach of movie product placements, including presence in new international markets and consumer sectors and, through a demand effect, potentially increased stockage in hotel, restaurant or airline bars as more people begin to ask for the beer.

Storytelling ads can connect with other stories in the audience's experience by referring intertextually to news media stories and causes, such as the Nike campaign that cast former NFL star Colin Kaepernick relating part of his experience of anti-racist activism. In that campaign, Nike struck a similarly radical and politically progressive tone to that of their first iconic ad, Revolution[50] (discussed earlier). Advertising stories are not always unifying, they can be divisive, as is the case with many controversial ads (including some of Nike's campaigns and the notorious Benetton campaigns of the 1990s[51]). Of course, there is also political advertising, such as many promoted stories and advertisements in British mainstream and social media about leaving the EU (or Brexit), which divided the UK roughly down the middle of the population, judging by the outcome of the EU referendum.[52] Controversial ads can generate tumultuous responses on social media, but as Benetton discovered, this only benefits the cause when there are supporters as well as opponents. Oliviero Toscani's last campaign as chief of Benetton advertising was one based on life-term prisoners called 'Death Row', and the backlash from some of the victims of the prisoners' crimes created too much heat for the brand. Toscani maintained that 'Death Row' was his best work for the brand.[53]

NARRATIVE TRANSPORTATION AND BRAND STORIES

There is something compelling and universal about stories per se that invites attention, but there can be little doubt that particular stories are more absorbing than others. One way of conceptualising different levels of reader engagement with stories is through the idea of narrative transportation, the extent to which a reader becomes deeply absorbed in a story and is, in effect, transported in their imagination by the story. Researchers have found that this effect is not only present with traditional story forms, but also with advertisements.[54] While cognitive research has conceived of narrative transportation in ads as a route to persuasion, it is clearly an odd thing to suppose that one can become carried away in one's imagination by a story that you know has been written simply to sell you something. Barbara Phillips and Edward McQuarrie[55] found in their research that different types of creative execution elicited different responses from readers who might engage with the ad to identify, to act, to feel, or to become immersed in the ad, or imaginatively transported by it. They found that transportation and immersion persuaded the reader by intensifying the experience of the brand and, through that, creating a positive frisson around the brand. This has a brand building effect, creating the 'mental availability' that, according to Byron Sharp, results in market share.

Advertisements, then, are able to elicit the same kinds of response from readers as other story forms, although by no means are all ads storytelling ads, and by no means are all consumer/readers predisposed to becoming absorbed in the story portrayed in an ad. As the category 'advertising' blurs into the category 'media content' it seems that more and more advertising content falls into the storytelling category. This might be a consequence, or an effect, of the narrowing gap between the advertising and entertainment industries, or it might be a strategic shift as big brands realise that programmatic social media and search advertising cannot build brands and develop audience reach.

In one sense, the advertising industry has not changed – creative ads that are worth watching tend to leverage valuable publicity for brands, as they have always done. But, although the idea of storytelling has taken hold in an industry logic, it can be difficult to tell stories through paratexts. Rather, paratexts tend to inflect other, bigger stories and to cue ways in which those bigger stories can be read. That is, on the face of it, paratexual brand advertising content does not necessarily lend itself easily to the narrative trajectories of conventional storytelling. Narrative transportation effects are probably not evoked by a discarded McDonald's wrapper (although they might, if the wrapper evinces a memory in one's life). Of course, we can say that brands now supply spaces into which consumers can inscribe their own preferred meanings, but are there rules that apply that constrain or frame the meanings that can be drawn from particular patterns of brand paratexts? Have the rules of media poetics changed in a post-digital age dominated by paratexts?

Recent research on the narrative transportation effect in advertisements by Feiereisen and colleagues and by Tom van Lear and colleagues[56] has suggested that, while it is possible for advertisements (aka brand content) to elicit narrative transportation, consumers engage in different ways with different types of advertising text, transportation being only one of the possible forms of engagement.[57] Citing Roland Barthes,[58] Feiereisen and colleagues mention the fetishist who savours particular phrases and quotes, the obsessional and paranoid readers who engage in detailed close reading of the text to the point of seeking out 'hidden' meanings, and the enthusiast who abandons critical reading in favour of deep immersion in the text. There are also mechanical considerations, whereby some readers favour top-down scanning of a text while others favour selective interjection into the text or favour a bottom-up approach (like newspaper readers who start with the sports pages at the back), and also social contexts: some readers engage with brand texts as members of fan communities, while others may be reading from a different motive. Feiereisen and colleagues develop a number of nuanced narrative positions from these reading strategies. We have previously noted Iser's location of the meaning of a text in the space between text and reader, but we can now see this space becoming bigger and more complex under the forces of media convergence.

Feiereisen and colleagues focused their study on how consumers negotiate their engagement with the primary text of a media brand such as a movie via the many iterations of that brand across various media platforms, and they suggest that the idea of a single authorial voice controlling a cohesive narrative is redundant now that consumers are empowered through the technologies of media delivery to manage their own narrative trajectory through brand stories. The loss of linearity in the consumption of brand stories means that each brand text occupies a space that is inherently relational in that it interacts with multiple other texts in the reader's universe. In their focus on media brands and transmedia storytelling, Feiereisen and colleagues' analysis moves closer towards the paratextual analyses of film and TV scholars such as Jonathan Gray who in his book, *Show Sold Separately,*[59] examines the relations of movie and TV show promotional paratexts, and all the associated epitextual content such as fan wikis. Like Gennette, though, Feiereisen and colleagues maintain a hierarchical relation between primary text and secondary text, such as that between the primary text of the brand narrative and the secondary texts of, say, fan fiction. This does not preclude readers from changing the narrative entirely, as in fan fiction, or with the James Bond stories written and filmed after Ian Fleming's death, but the narrative brand (as opposed to the brand narrative) retains its logical primacy. Feiereisen and colleagues also posit the non-narrative brand in this primary position, while acknowledging that the circulation of what they describe as transmedia content (i.e. brand paratexts) inflects the meaning of the primary text.

We discuss the papers above at some length because they illustrate the trajectory of business school literary research into advertising and point to directions for brand management practice in an age of widespread and immersive media consumption. The above research illustrates the vitality and variety of consumers' reading and engagement strategies with narrative brands. In contrast to the above research, our paratextual perspective suggests that a hierarchical relation of primary to secondary text can be abandoned, and the brand narrative can be conceived as text without content, until that content is inscribed into it by its paratexts. As we have tried to illustrate with many examples in this book, this does not mean that the kinetic dynamism of brand representations and intertexts across media platforms acts to create a meaningless hall of mirrors. What makes a brand a brand is its recognisability as an entity in spite of the variety of its representations.

CONCLUDING COMMENTS

In Chapter 6 we have discussed some of the different ways in which brand texts might be accessed, curated and read by consumers, and we have touched on some of the implications for brand meaning and its management. Leaving open the many questions that still persist around the topic, we hope that the chapter demonstrated a connecting theme – that is, our contention that neither brands nor advertisements constitute stories in the literary sense. Rather, the brand is an unwritten story the elements of which are inferred by audiences from the paratexts they access. There is then, perhaps, no need for close analyses of the socio-semiotic mechanics of the reading process. Perhaps it is enough to understand that, as with literary works, there is no definitive narrative of the brand, its meanings reside in the space between text and reader.

In Chapter 7 we will turn to the managerial practicalities of the para-textual perspective on brands and communication. Given all we have discussed up this point, how might brand and advertising management respond, considering the current existential crisis of the advertising industry and the dominance of the big digital platforms over media consumption?

NOTES

1. True Move H, Giving is the best communication TV spot: https://www.youtube.com/watch?v=7s22HX18wDY
2. Vizer ad, Thailand: https://www.youtube.com/watch?v=S-fvxEq_3DA
3. Barbara J. Phillips and Edward F. McQuarrie, Narrative and persuasion in fashion advertising. *Journal of Consumer Research*, 37(3) (October 2010) 368–392. DOI: 10.1086/653087.
4. https://chertseymuseum.org/Holloway
5. And later to earn even more distinction by appointing a Hackley family member as its inaugural Chair in Marketing.
6. Perhaps Simon Cowell might consider sponsoring the P. T. Barnum School of Business Communication at Royal Hollloway?
7. See Stephen Brown and Chris Hackley, The Greatest Showman on Earth: Is Simon Cowell P.T. Barnum reborn? *Journal of Historical Research in Marketing*, 4(2) (2012) 290. DOI: 10.1108/17557501211224467.
8. See, for example, this search for nursery rhyme themed ads: https://www.google.com/search?q=ads+with+nursery+rhymes&safe=strict&client=firefox-b-d&source=lnms&tbm=isch&sa=X&ved=2ahUKEwjR1f2i6sLxAhW3QkEAHfqKCawQ_AUoAXoECAEQAw&biw=758&bih=722
9. https://www.thetimes.co.uk/article/what-ever-happened-to-the-oxo-family-fhm6jjn097q
10. Here's the Oxo Christmas ad from 1984: https://www.youtube.com/watch?v=EQXxbW7qYFQ
11. https://www.manchestereveningnews.co.uk/news/greater-manchester-news/iconic-oxo-advert-salford-mum-12007371
12. https://www.youtube.com/watch?v=jsN4YwbM9kw
13. This is one from 2017 – The Escape: https://www.youtube.com/watch?v=qnUicdd8wnE
14. See Rungpaka Amy Tiwsakul and Christopher Hackley, Young Thai and UK consumers' experiences of television product placement – engagement, resistance and objectification, in Margaret Craig Lees, Teresa Davis, and Gary Gregory (Eds) *Asia-Pacific Advances in Consumer Research Volume*

7 (2006), Association for Consumer Research, pp. 372–377. Available at: https://www.acrwebsite.org/volumes/ap07/12969.pdf

15. One of the authors helped a journalist in this UK newspaper piece about movie product placement: https://www.mirror.co.uk/lifestyle/going-out/film/superman-film-man-steel-rakes-1947071

16. The definitive Ehrenberg et al. paper in advertising as publicity is discussed by Byron Sharp here: https://www.marketingscience.info/wp-content/uploads/2021/10/Ehrenbergs-Views-on-Advertising.pdf

17. Paul Feldwick illustrates this point in his book *Why Does the Pedlar Sing? What Creativity Really Means in Advertising*, published by Troubadour, in which he argues that creative and successful advertising tends to be entertaining.

18. See Feldwick's piece on advertising and entertainment here: https://bristolcreativeindustries.com/importance-of-entertainment-in-advertising/

19. https://greekgodsandgoddesses.net/goddesses/nike/

20. https://creative.starbucks.com/logos/

21. https://www.mashed.com/142329/the-untold-truth-of-starbucks/

22. See, for example, these great examples of myth-driven poster advertising from the early 1900s: https://gizmodo.com/13-ads-that-feature-mythical-gods-selling-modern-produc-882484658

23. See Chris Hackley, Rungpaka Amy Hackley and Dina H. Bassiouni, Imaginary futures: Liminoid advertising and consumer identity. *Journal of Marketing Communications*, 27(3) (2021) 269–283. DOI: 10.1080/13527266.2019.1694564.

24. Fabletics – a new year, a new you: https://www.youtube.com/watch?v=nOJdm79a8II

25. https://www.thenewyouplan.com/

26. https://www.a-newyou.co.uk/

27. See Victor Turner, *The Ritual Process: Structure and Anti-Structure* (2017; first published 1969), Routledge.

28. Arnold van Gennep, *The Rites of Passage*, 2nd Edition (2019), University of Chicago Press.

29. See Chris Hackley, Stephen Brown and Rungpaka Amy Hackley, The *X Factor* enigma: Simon Cowell and the marketization of existential liminality. *Marketing Theory*, 12(4) (2012) 451–469. DOI: 10.1177/1470593112457738.

30. Chris Hackley and Rungpaka Amy Hackley, Marketing and the cultural production of celebrity in the convergent media era. *Journal of Marketing Management*, 31(5/6) (2015) 461–477. http://www.tandfonline.com/doi/full/10.1080/0267257X.2014.1000940

31. Joseph Campbell, *The Hero With a Thousand Faces*. https://www.jcf.org/works/titles/the-hero-with-a-thousand-faces/

32. Campbell's Hero's Journey and advertising: http://www.thearetical.com/blog/the-heros-journey-in-advertising

33. https://econsultancy.com/five-travel-and-tourism-marketing-campaigns-2019-emotional-storytelling/

34. See S.M.A. Moin, Sameer Hosany and Justin O'Brien, Storytelling in desti-nation brands' promotional videos. *Tourism Management Perspectives*, 34 (2020). DOI: 10.1016/j.tmp.2020.100639. https://www.sciencedirect.com/ science/article/abs/pii/S2211973620300064?via%3Dihub#ab0010

35. For example, David Puttnam (see https://www.independent.co.uk/news/ people/profiles/passed-failed-an-education-in-the-life-of-david-puttnam -film-producer-and-open-university-chancellor-394929.html), Michael Cimino, Tony and Ridley Scott, Alan Parker, Jonathan Glazer (see https:// doddlenews.com/directors-who-started-by-making-commercials-part-1/), not to mention Michael Bay, David Fincher, Guillermo del Torro, Edgar Wright and, as an example of a director who went back to ads after becom-ing established in movies, David Lynch (see https://www.businessinsider .com/ads-by-directors-before-they-were-famous-2013-7?r=US&IR=T).

36. See Paul Grainge and Catherine Johnson, *The Promotional Screen Industries* (2015), Routledge.

37. Chloe Preece, Finola Kerrigan and Daragh O'Reilly, License to assemble: Theorizing brand longevity. *Journal of Consumer Research*, 46(2) (August 2019) 330–350. DOI: 10.1093/jcr/ucy076.

38. For an account of Bond authors see: https://www.empireonline.com/movies/ features/james-bond-literary-afterlife/

39. For an account of Bond watches see https://manofmany.com/fashion/ watches/a-complete-list-of-all-the-james-bond-watches

40. https://www.forbes.com/sites/travisbean/2020/04/18/all-26-james-bond -films-ranked-at-the-box-office/?sh=377b78f91804

41. This is a very nice account of product placement in Bond movies: https:// blog.hollywoodbranded.com/blog/james-bond-product-placement-the -definitive-timeline-of-brands-in-bond

42. Rosemary J. Avery and Rosellina Ferraro, Verisimilitude or advertising? Brand appearances on prime-time television. *The Journal of Consumer Affairs*, 34(2) (2000) 217–244. Accessed 8 July 2021. *JSTOR*: www.jstor .org/stable/23860042

43. https://kotaku.com/i-m-sorry-to-say-laurence-fishburne-died-in-the-2005 -ma-1844803953

44. Stephanie Feiereisen, Dina Rasolofoarison, Crystal Russell and Hope Jensen Schau, One brand, many trajectories: Narrative navigation in transmedia. *Journal of Consumer Research*, 48(4) (2020) 651–681. DOI: 10.1093/jcr/ ucaa046.

45. Stephen Brown, Pierre McDonagh and Clifford J. Shultz, II, *Titanic*: Consuming the myths and meanings of an ambiguous brand. *Journal of Consumer Research*, 40(4) (1 December 2013) 595–614. DOI: 10.1086/671474.

46. https://www.comparethemarket.com/?AFFCLIE=FV67&SRC= FV67&cmpid=PC-_-GOG-_-AL-_-MKT-_-haNFMywalaePBBC& ds_rl=1251650&ds_rl=1251650&gclid=EAIaIQobChMI67HCgen p8QIVwbTtCh2sUQ8wEAAYASAAEgJ2P_D_BwE&gclsrc=aw.ds

47. On visual memory: https://www.theguardian.com/lifeandstyle/2016/dec/18/ pictures-trigger-memories-faster-than-words-neuroscientist

48. Marcel Proust on the Madeleine object, from *Remembrance of Things Past*: http://art.arts.usf.edu/content/articlefiles/2330-Excerpt%20from %20Remembrance%20of%20Things%20Past%20by%20Marcel%20Proust .pdf

49. On objects and personal narrative: https://www.nature.com/articles/s41598 -018-35899-y

50. As we discuss earlier, referring to Alan Bradshaw and Linda Scott's book on the subject, *Advertising Revolution* (referenced earlier, but in case you missed it, published by Repeater books: https://www.penguinrandomhouse .com/books/577405/advertising-revolution-by-alan-bradshaw/#).

51. https://www.vogue.co.uk/gallery/benettons-best-advertising-campaigns

52. https://www.bbc.co.uk/news/politics/eu_referendum/results

53. http://www.ericjlyman.com/adageglobal.html

54. For example, Jennifer Edson Escalas, Self-referencing and persuasion: Narrative transportation versus analytical elaboration. *Journal of Consumer Research*, 33(4) (2007) 421–429. DOI: 10.1086/510216. Jing Wang and Bobby J. Calder, Media transportation and advertising. *Journal of Consumer Research*, 33(2) (2006) 151–162. DOI: 10.1086/506296.

55. Barbara J. Phillips and Edward F. McQuarrie, Narrative and persuasion in fashion advertising. *Journal of Consumer Research*, 37(3) (2010) 368–392. DOI: 10.1086/653087.

56. Tom van Laer, Stephanie Feiereisen and Luca M. Visconti, Storytelling in the digital era: A meta-analysis of relevant moderators of the narrative trans-portation effect. *Journal of Business Research*, 96(1) (2019) 135–146. DOI: 10.2139/ssrn.3156933. Available at: https://ssrn.com/abstract=3156933

57. Tom van Laer, Ko de Ruyter, Luca M. Visconti and Martin Wetzels, The extended transportation-imagery model: A meta-analysis of the anteced-ents and consequences of consumers' narrative transportation. *Journal of Consumer Research*, 40(5) (2014) 797–817. DOI: 10.1086/673383.

58. Roland Barthes, *S/Z*, trans. Richard Miller (1975), Cape.

59. Jonathan Gray, *Show Sold Separately: Promos, Spoilers, and Other Media Paratexts* (2010), New York University Press.

7. Paratextual advertising strategy

INTRODUCTION

In Chapter 7 we explore the practical implications of our paratextual perspective on promotion. We offer no apologies or caveats for this; it is merely the convention of management books. In any case, it would seem perverse to argue for a paratextual understanding of the practical discipline of advertising without any consideration of how a paratextual understanding might be applied. Indeed, one of our key motivations for writing this book is that we feel that a stronger intellectual grasp of the reading processes entailed in advertising potentially benefits all stakeholders, including brand managers, ad agencies and the public.

We will begin with a brief account of how advertising gets made, in order to try to set a solid foundation for the changes implied in the paratextual perspective. After that, we will offer some suggestions about how paratextual branding and advertising strategies might play out.

PRESSURES ON THE CREATIVE AGENCY SYSTEM

There are two ways to make an ad – the right way, and all the other ways. We talk about both at length in our book *Advertising and Promotion*, referenced previously. For now, we want to provide a brief sketch of the creative advertising development process as a baseline from which to nuance this process for a media-agnostic and digitally saturated consumer environment. It is necessary as a caveat to say that doing advertising the right way demands certain preconditions and resources (that is, money, time and client trust) that are increasingly difficult for ad agencies to acquire. We have said earlier that the creative agency system is undergoing an existential crisis. This crisis has many elements, all of which conspire to press clients into superficially easy and often digital platform-driven solutions that are not sufficiently thrashed out with research, reasoning and creative input. There are financial and time pressures that can lead to rushed conclusions.

One of the reasons for this is the rapid growth of search and social advertising, which advertisers can commission and plan without any help from an ad agency. The very broad category of digital advertising, including video content, display and banner, and many other types in addition to search and social, now takes just over half of all global adspend (the total amount of money spent on advertising annually). The pace of the shift in ad budgets from traditional advertising (print, TV, radio, outdoor) to digital has been accelerated by COVID-19. However, total global adspend is around $US650 billion per year[1] at the time of writing (late 2021), so just under half of that is still a very big number, more than enough to sustain a vibrant creative ad agency system.

This is not to imply that creative agencies can only make ads for traditional media – it is an article of faith in marketing communication that campaigns are usually *integrated*, or, TTL (through the line), meaning they run executions across different media channels and platforms, both traditional and digital, as part of the same campaign. Even single ads often have multi-platform executions, for example where a campaign might include a TV spot, a version of the TV ad for owned and social media, stills from the ad for print and outdoor (or Out Of Home) ads, and a jingle that can be recognised in radio or podcast ads. Creative ideas have to be spreadable across media channels and platforms, so there is no clear line between traditional and digital advertising for the agencies. But the vast advertising revenues of the digital platforms rest on the idea that advertising can be reduced to an arm of behavioural economics, driven by big data and big surveillance, and popping up on users' phones or tablets at moments of convenience and vulnerability. We do not question the value of search and social advertising, particularly for smaller, local businesses, but we strongly reject the idea that it renders traditional creative advertising and the development process redundant or outdated, for reasons that we will examine below.

So, making ads today is about generating ideas that 'have legs' and can be applied flexibly in different kinds of execution. This demands a broader skill set than in decades past when advertising creatives could make a name for themselves by being specialists in one channel (TV, radio, etc.) or even in one type of execution on one channel. For example, legendary creative John Webster of London agency BMP[2] was hardly a one trick pony[3] but he was best known for creating famous brand characters for TV spots of the 1970s, 1980s and 1990s, including the Sugar

Puffs Honey Monster (according to anecdote an idea borrowed from the Andy Williams show), the Hofmeister Bear who changed drinking culture in the UK (and not for the better), the Cadbury's Smash Martians who were amazed that humans ate anything as primitive as real potatoes, the cool and funky Cresta Polar Bear and, later changing creative tack, ads that featured celebrities such as footballer Gary Lineker and comedian Jack Dee.[4] It seems almost impossible today for an ad agency creative to generate a reputation like Webster's because the game has fundamentally changed, not to mention the budgets. Ad agencies are fighting for business, cutting costs and offering clients multi-platform campaigns that will (clients hope) deliver everything at great value. The client holding a brief for a big budget TV spot with full creative rein given over to the agency is a rare bird these days. Besides, making ads today is deeply collaborative and it is increasingly difficult for anyone on the account team to definitively say 'that was my idea'.[5] Advertising creatives today are not temperamental maverick geniuses but collaborative members of a multi-skilled team.[6]

Not only are technology, the big digital platforms and changing work practices squeezing the space in which ad agencies operate, but so are other institutions such as brand consultancies, in-house operations, media agencies and BTL (below the line) specialists, all of whom see no reason why they can't make big budget creative ads just as well as the big ad agencies. After all, only the biggest full-service ad agencies still keep full movie production units on the payroll. There are more than enough jobbing writers, casting agents, film directors and camera crews sitting around to hire them in for the job if a client signs a cheque for a TV spot. The same goes for full digital roll-outs, app design, advergames, content: you name it, the expertise can be bought in. Buying in specialised talent is cost-efficient in a time of shrinking budgets and transactional business relationships. At least, that's the way ad making is sometimes done. As a result of all these pressures, the idea of ad making as a strategic skill based on accumulated experience and knowledge – and preserved in the hallowed corridors of the great creative agencies – tends to be sidelined.

THE ART OF MAKING GOOD ADVERTISEMENTS

The problem for ad agencies is that myths abound about the best way to make good ads, and when advertising is done badly the reasons for the failure are quickly forgotten. An ad that is put together without a clear analysis of the reason for advertising, that is, the marketing benefit of advertising, grounded in careful market and consumer research, along with nuanced and insight-based creative, and a clear idea of what the audience needs to think/feel/or do as a result of seeing the ad, is quite unlikely to have a clearly conceived set of objectives against which to measure its effectiveness. If it fails, the evidence is scant, and likely to remain confidential. There are so many bad ads because the marketing industry has no institutional memory for them. If bridges fall down then civil engineers analyse why, so they can build ones that stay up, but the ad industry has no such consensus on methods and lacks such a vivid accountability. There are lists of advertising disasters, 'banned' ads and advertising howlers out there on the web, but these tend to be anecdotal. There exist stocks of advertising case histories that document successful campaigns,[7] but the particularity of each successful advertising campaign tends to resist attempts to systematise and codify the process. Besides, there is a self-confirming bias present in ad industry award winners – if the process is being documented as part of a case study for submission to a major award, then the presence of the process will increase the likelihood of success.

Notwithstanding the elusiveness of a formula for successful advertising, there have been some principles of practice that appeal for their documented record of success, and for their elegance. The process is not a necessary precondition for successful creative advertising development: it is an attempt to distil what seem to be the common and replicable elements of successful ads. We base our understanding of this process on 20 years of research into the creative advertising development process in leading agencies, beginning with the first author's PhD, which involved conversations with advertising professionals in all account team roles in London agencies in the 1990s,[8] especially the legendary creative agency BMP DDB and its innovation of the account planning system,[9] and extending subsequently to research in US and UK advertising and media agencies, and, through the second author's PhD and subsequent research, Asian and UK advertising, media and product placement agencies.[10] We emphasise this process because the history of how great ads were created seems to have been forgotten in some quarters of the industry.

By 'account team' below we mean the traditional arrangement of advertising development into a team consisting of client services/account management, account planning/strategy, creative. So, with apologies for the lengthy preamble, and also for the oversimplicity of what follows, we feel (based on our research) that the best way to make good advertising goes something like this:

1. The pitch won, the account is given to an account team (or to several account teams on a big account) and the client brief is converted to a communications brief. This is because marketing objectives and communications objectives are not the same: advertising has to be based on an understanding of how communication can support marketing objectives. The conflation of communication with marketing objectives is one of the most common flaws in how advertising is conceived.

2. Initial research is conducted, usually from secondary sources but sometimes supplemented by qualitative work, into the market, the target audience, the sector and the brand. The aim is to understand what this brand, and this consumption practice, means in the lived experience of consumers. At this stage, there will be a clear understanding of the budget constraints and the probable media.

3. The communication and advertising strategy are devised. These dovetail into each other. The ad strategy concerns what the viewer must think, feel or do as a result of seeing the ad: the communications strategy must refer to how communication in the campaign overall can support the client's marketing objective. There should be clear and simple (though perhaps ingenious) objectives for each. Media decisions should be finalised.

4. The creative brief is written and signed off by all parties and the creative execution is devised. This is how the ad design will deliver on the advertising strategy, and it refers to what the ad (or ads in a multi-platform campaign) will look, sound and feel like. This is the creative part, in the sense that creative decisions have to be made that will embed the purpose into the ad design. Many of the best (that is, the most effective) creative executions have been grounded in qualitative insight into the audience's cultural milieu, behaviour and thinking. The ad must speak to its target audience by being relevant, and there must be a good reason why the audience will find the ad plausibly relevant. The kind of insight this requires is not behavioural insight, but psycho-cultural insight.

5. Production, pre-testing, creative iteration if needed, media planning and roll-out.

6. Additional considerations may be the design and coordination of multiple iterations of the creative across different platforms and channels.

7. Monitoring and feedback processes have to be in place during the campaign.

Simplistic and generalised though this sequence is, we feel that it represents the nearest thing the industry has to a formalised process of creative advertising development.

THREATS TO THE ACCOUNT TEAM SYSTEM

The idea of the account team as the fundamental unit of traditional advertising development, though, may be fading away, and, with it, the sense of a logical process of creative advertising development that fits around defined roles. There are, we speculate, two main reasons for this. Firstly, the process is easily misunderstood and reified into a tick-box caricature, and there are no longer enough people in the industry with the experience of it to remind everyone how it actually works. In particular, the sense of linearity in the process is only present on paper. When it is done professionally there are constant conversations, iteration and feedback loops throughout the process. The account team is a team. However, when the process is conducted naïvely it can be seen as a 'baton-passing' process in which the parties do not need to constantly interact. Like most work processes, the social context is fundamental to efficiency and effectiveness. If account team members are not constantly liaising throughout every step in the process, it doesn't work. The stock response to this problem is to impose open-plan offices in the hope that this forces everyone to talk to each other, but this also has its drawbacks. People need private space to think as well as social space to interact. There has to be quiet as well as noise.

The second main reason for the weakening of the account team system is that teams need to be bigger in order to embrace a greater range of expertise. Creative ideas have to be executed across many different platforms. Doing this takes not only creative craft skills but technical skills, so people have to be on hand who can say what will work on this or that platform, and what won't. Buying in technical expertise won't quite wash – the expertise needs to be in at the start of the process to contribute to the development of the ad and communication strategy. From the simple expedient of adding a digital planner to the account team in the 2000s, big agencies have found that they need a larger pool of expertise throughout the process, hence the coherence and coordination of the tight account team group is weakened.

Not only is there a need for a deep understanding of how creative ideas will work across digital technologies, but even the traditional sub-disciplines of advertising (the 'promotional mix') are collapsing into each other. For example, where does TV advertising end and Public Relations (PR) begin when the major goals of the ad will inevitably include generating earned media coverage such as social media shares, coverage in the business press, and consumer comment, memes and parodies? Earlier we discussed how digital platforms are enabling hybrid advertising genres to emerge that combine a number of the elements of the old promotional mix. PR, sponsorship, content, advertising, celebrity endorsement and UGC (User Generated Content) have porous borders when they are executed across digital platforms. This means all the disciplines have to be in the team right from the client brief.

This collision of promotional disciplines in the advertising industry is expressed well in Paul Grainge and Catherine Johnson's research-based book *Promotional Screen Industries*.[11] Grainge and Johnson detail a London agency, Red Bee, that originated as an in-house BBC video production unit specialising in feature trailers and channel promotions such as idents and interstitials. Red Bee became an independent advertising, production and media business with creative[12] and media[13] divisions.

Red Bee's evolution reflects the new reality that advertising development can no longer act as if it spins off the centrifugal force of a prime-time TV spot. Ad agencies once claimed to be media neutral while still thinking in the traditional way about TV being the big circus ring for advertising: today, digital media tend to be the focus for clients. Complicating the issue is the fact that, while digital media can sometimes deliver extraordinarily large audiences at minimal cost with, for example, video content that goes viral, TV can, still, deliver impact even though real-time TV audiences have shrunk considerably and persistently for the past 40 years.

So, making advertising needs to have everything it always needed: a sense of the reason for advertising, a sense of what the ad (ads) must do, and a connection between the advertising strategy and the client's marketing objective. But, it is more difficult to generate a coherent sense of strategy in large multi-disciplinary teams than it once was in the three-discipline account team. There is a strong argument that the traditional creative advertising development process simply no longer makes sense for multi-platform, creatively integrated campaigns run by large, multi-disciplinary teams. The traditional creative advertising development process worked for an account team of four or five people, with others working on the periphery. The distinction between those at the centre of the process, and those who occupy lower ranks in the hierarchy, is more difficult to sustain with bigger teams, more egos, less agency authority and more client power. Clients today often expect, or demand, to be creative partners in the development of advertising. This can be problematic for agencies who have to persuade clients that communication is a specialism with different craft skills to marketing. In addition, the correct advertising solution might be counterintuitive and is not always palatable for clients who have their own battles to fight in their own boardrooms. Agencies who are seen by clients as mere service providers rather than strategic partners have great difficulty in making the case that they add real value for clients.[14] All these factors mean that making good advertising is more difficult and complicated than in the days when the big creative agencies ruled by consent.

CONFLICTING ASSUMPTIONS ABOUT HOW ADS WORK

We need to briefly return to the question of how advertising works, because the differing, implicit assumptions that different players bring to the ad development process can have a huge impact on the outcome.[15] We know that an AI[16] machine can tweak a search or social ad in AB testing to double its CTR from 0.8% to 1.6%. This is not creativity; it is incrementally increased effectiveness driven by real-time behaviour data. The idea that personalisation was the holy grail of advertising has receded as the data have made the truth clear – this is not how advertising works best, because advertising is not personal selling. Earlier in the book we mention the line of ideas of Andrew Ehrenberg through to Byron Sharp.[17] Ehrenberg and colleagues realised that mass media advertising operates by generating publicity for the brand (or for whatever else is being advertised). Advertising does not operate as salesmanship in print, in John E Kennedy's overused aphorism, because it is a mediated communication. Advertising rarely persuades us to buy stuff. It puts ideas in our heads that, might, predispose us to buy stuff. In more long-winded terms, advertising creates a cultural presence for a brand, making it seem relevant, interesting and memorable. Sales inevitably follow when this is done well, because a lot of people will think of the brand when they think of the category. What matters, using Byron Sharp's terminology, is for advertising to create 'mental availability' for a brand by making distinctive advertising that contains brand assets; that is, things that make clear what brand is advertising.

As former planning chief of BMP Paul Feldwick[18] explains, this means that an advertisement does not have to contain a coherent message as such (even though the explicit, differentiating sales message remains an article of faith in 120 years of business school advertising research and theory).[19] The ad just needs to be distinctive, even if the association of the brand asset with the brand isn't rational ('Whassup?', 'It's the Milky Bar Kid', 'I'm Lovin' It', the Sugar Puffs Honey Monster, the comparethe-market.com meerkats and countless others). In fact, the less rational, the better. Feldwick refers to a fame model of advertising – ads have to get famous, and by so doing they make the brand famous.[20] Being entertaining is a useful route to fame.

Importantly, targeting and segmentation, two of the pillars of the mindshare model of advertising, are not necessarily very important. Ads that are seen by people who will never buy the brand can, in fact, be very useful. Why else would *The Sun*, the UK tabloid catering mainly for a C2DE[21] readership (semi- and unskilled workers and those unemployed[22]) and written for a reading age of about eight years old,[23] carry a lengthy promotional review of a car that costs more than half a million US dollars?[24] Granted, there is a potential market there of premiership footballers and self-made plumbing magnates, but the broader truth is that drivers of prestige cars want the general public to recognise the brand they drive and to know how much it cost. It is useful to brands to cultivate a cultural presence. Luxury brands, in particular, are a currency of prestige that requires wide recognition.

The greatest ad campaigns, then, became famous because a lot of people noticed and enjoyed them who had not thought about the brand before or who had thought of it and didn't care about it either before or after viewing it. The ads were intrinsically striking and/or entertaining to a wide audience. As Byron Sharp maintains, the highest consumer market shares usually result not from a clot of frequent repeat purchasers (the mythical 'loyal' brand consumers), but from a much larger number of occasional casual purchasers. The leading market shares are usually sustained by ads that consistently keep a brand amongst the two or three in each category that most people can easily remember, provided those brands are also convenient to buy. The convenience is important – retail opportunities, product ranges, service, financing and the other marketing elements have to be lined up in order for the ads to do their work.

It is a matter of legend in the ad business that ads that are entertaining but do not sell product irritate clients. But this idea needs picking apart. If an ad is truly entertaining then, provided the media coverage was adequate, the brand gained some exposure. This is not necessarily a bad thing. Was the ad strategy thought through? Were the sales projections unrealistic given the budget? Was the product no good or the retail coverage uneven? There could be many reasons why ad campaigns fail, but it is hard to follow the reasoning that an ad lots of people enjoyed was of no benefit to the client. Unless it was simply a poor attempt to entertain and failed on its own terms by not being very entertaining.

So, there are divergent assumptions about how advertising works, and the bigger and more diverse the account team group must be, the more divergent the assumptions. There has to be some kind of accommodation between the old saws of creative advertising, with the more pragmatic and data-driven wisdom of the newer digital genres of advertising. How do such quaint ideas about entertaining ads translate in an advertising world in which account teams are diffused across multiple disciplines, providers and egos, media neutrality is a given, TV spots are no longer the fulcrum around which the ad world turns, and ad strategy is, it seems, almost a forgotten discipline?

DOING PARATEXTUAL ADVERTISING STRATEGICALLY

Doing paratextual advertising strategically is a three-dimensional game that has to consider the trajectories of brand presence as they appear in the context of the audiences' lived experiences.[25] This might be thought of as mapping brand meanings as they coalesce in momentary assemblages, as Chloe Preece and colleagues theorised with regard to the Bond movie franchise[26] (discussed in Chapter 6). Or, continuing the film performance analogy, it might entail considering the holistic *mise en scène* of the brand as it appears in its full kinaesthetic context.[27] The major functional implication of this holistic approach is that there has to be a planning-led understanding of the brand, adapted and extended to suit the demands of the convergence era. We use the term audiences rather than consumers because, as we have discussed above, brands, for the purposes of communication strategy, must be understood as communication phenomena within a seamless media landscape. They are understood and encountered on the same plane as all the other genres of media content that media users consume, and therefore must compete with those other forms of content for attention. The contextual approach to paratextual brand and advertising strategy, we suggest, is informed by an agnostic but holistic understanding of the full range and capabilities of the media channels and platforms that are available to relevant audiences. The approach is semantically nuanced through a wide and deep appreciation of topical affairs and consumer cultures and sub-cultures, and it is driven by strategically framed and insight-mediated creativity.

So, what we claim follows from our paratextual perspective is that the principles of good advertising management haven't changed at all, yet the context in which they have to be executed has changed completely. Advertising strategy still demands a planning mentality, by which we mean a mentality that considers the full complexity of the managerial problem, the situation and the potential solutions. This also implies that good advertising is not produced to a formula. It demands the nuanced judgements and persuasive rhetorical skills of people who possess flexible and furnished minds and a wide understanding of media technologies and platforms, and insight into the ways different audiences consume these media.

We aver, then, that digital platforms have not changed one particular thing about advertising – it still makes a difference whether an ad is good, or bad. Good ads, generally speaking, will do better than bad ones, and good means the ad is fun/interesting/informative enough for an audience to notice and react to it. It is important to remember that advertising strategy under media convergence is a continuum, running from inspiration to activation. The inspiration is the part that makes people think of and, maybe, remember or recognise the brand: the activation is the part that helps them to act on that thought. Personalised search and social ads are very good at activation, even though, like any other kind of advertising, their success is not the result of persuasion, but of audience reach. A 1% CTR is only meaningful either when it is 1% of a very big number, or when the advertising firm is a small, local operation. Search and social ads can be especially powerful for small businesses and sole traders because of the value they represent, and for larger operations who need to turn mental availability into sales. Personalised ads are most powerful when they can leverage the capital earned by a mass audience campaign for the brand.

The campaign must lead with a clear sense of strategy, and this has to be informed by a thorough understanding of the brand, the market, the consumers and the wider potential audiences. What does the client need to accomplish, and how can communication facilitate this? The basis for strategic thinking clearly has to be much broader than in the Mad Men days because large audiences can now be reached by channels other than TV, and at a far lower relative cost per person reached. It would seem logical for a smallish team to take charge of strategy development, in concert with discussions as necessary with the wider team. When brands take their eye off the ball and allow subcontracted agencies to interpret strategy, problems can occur. For example, the three-second 2017 Dove Facebook ad that was accused of being racist[28] challenged more than a decade's worth of positively received branding that promoted gender and racial equality (the incident also illustrated the power of paratexts to change the meaning of a brand when amplified through UGC on social media). Of course, there remain questions over whether negative PR lasts long enough to damage brands given the speed of the social media news cycle.[29]

Media agnosticism does not imply an aversion to TV. The UK comparethemarket.com meerkats' campaign, for example, began with a brief to find a search term that would be easy to remember, distinctive and good on organic search results. It turned out that the solution to this problem had huge creative potential. What began as a cheapish, low-level activation strategy ballooned into a full-blown creative campaign including lots of TV. One would assume that the entire meerkat storyworld was not what was envisioned at the initial planning stage. While the people at VCCP[30] might tell us differently, it would be surprising if there wasn't a good deal of unplanned creativity and a bit of blind luck behind this evolution as ideas begat other ideas.

In the old days, the movie production of TV ads was a key area where unplanned but ultimately useful elements of creative content emerged. Iconic, TV-led ads of the 1980s, 1990s and 2000s – such as Levi's Laundrette,[31] Guinness Surfers[32] and the peerless Sony Balls[33] – all had elements of serendipity and/or spontaneous ideas from the director during filming that helped make them the successes they became.[34] Legend has it that the Guinness surfers who starred in the iconic ad were local beach bums who happened to be waiting for waves when they were rudely interrupted by AMV's eager film production team. After all, advertising is a creative industry with creative people, and this is what happens. But the whole has to make sense as a whole, and strategy is the set of ideas that tie everything together under a sense of purpose. Without a clear sense of the overarching strategy or purpose of the ad, there wouldn't be the confidence to retain unexpected and emergent creative elements of the execution. These ads, 'heroic' ads in Google's tripartite division of content,[35] had to be filmic feasts of lavish entertainment, and the directors making them understood that this sometimes means spontaneous events make it into the final cut.

The hard part of multi-channel campaigns would be to ensure that the strategy remains at the core of creative executions that are operational-ised across multiple platforms. The Dove example above, for example, was a piece of lazy creativity that used an old and overused visual trope. Anyone with five years industry experience or a university education in advertising (or, indeed, pretty well anyone under 20 years old) ought to have seen the problem a mile off (although the black actress insisted that the ad was just misunderstood). But, big brands are big organisations that are not representative of the populations they serve, and issues do happen, from global car brands trying to sell rudely named cars in Brazil[36] to toy manufacturers getting it all wrong in China (the hapless Barbie[37]). These examples illustrate the age-old need for advertising strategists, planners and creatives, to have wide and deep cultural reference points along with topical sensitivity to the issues of the day, in order to consider the potential meanings of the creative execution. Back in the day, this meant people who dipped into the *Express* after they'd read *The Telegraph* and sometimes went to a football match. It means a rather more rigorous knowledge of popular consumer culture today. In 2021 the passenger on the Clapham omnibus has more computing power in their smartphone than it took to put the first man on the moon,[38] and while bouncing along Putney High Street on the number 39 they can browse their choice of the world's media output before alighting at Clapham Junction.

We admit that we love great creative ads and we are neglecting the more instrumental activation end of our paratextual advertising contin-uum. But we feel that the virtues of entertaining, creative advertising and those of TV have been neglected such is the noise around programmatic and personalisation. TV, though, has a different strategic role to the one it once had. TV now is one platform among many. We have mentioned examples of digital content that achieved audience reach many times greater than possible with TV, such as the multiple award-winning Epic Split,[39] a slickly produced marriage of a Hollywood actor and a Swedish car and truck brand that enhanced the fame of both[40] and, improbably, sold some trucks. Incidentally, one could imagine some brand executives being sniffy about associating their brand with an ageing B-movie actor known for low-concept, high-violence productions. The actor, though, is well known for having genuine martial arts skills, and his persona has acquired a tinge of self-mocking humour.[41]

The foregoing preamble leads, we hope, to a summary of the key points of paratextual advertising implementation. At the risk of adding to the inglorious canon of Ps (Place, Price, Product and Promotion), Cs (Consumer, Cost, Convenience and Communication), AIDAs (Attention, Interest, Desire, Action) and the other acronymic managerial marketing panaceas,[42] we offer the following guiding principles for paratextual advertising. A rudimentary rubric, if you will, for paratextual ad strategy. With the usual apologies and caveats, here are the five guiding principles we feel represent the practical implications of a paratextual perspective on advertising management.

PARATEXTUAL ADVERTISING – THE RUBRIC

1. **Content is advertising, and advertising is content.** Creative agencies have long been accused of seeing the world through TV advertising blinkers, and media neutrality was the buzz phrase that purported to address this relic of the commission payment era.[43] Distinctions between forms and genres of mediated branded content are not relevant to audiences in a seamless media landscape. Content is either worth attention, or it isn't. It is either perceived as authentic, or it isn't. Media agnosticism has to be a starting point for advertising strategy, the first question of which has to be 'what does the client need to accomplish that can be supported by communication?' This means that specialists who operate within platform and genre silos will still have their uses, but as suppliers of specialist expertise, not as strategists. This also implies that campaigns need to be led by a small team of strategists who have the planning skills and credibility to monitor the creative advertising development process through large-team, multi-disciplinary execution. Finally, it means that ad agencies do their best work as they always have, as cultural intermediaries,[44] latching on to cultural currents and mobilising these through creatively authentic content with which relevant audiences engage.[45]

2. **Flip the meaning hierarchy.** Any form of content can potentially become a dominant reading of the brand. A piece of serendipitously viral UGC (e.g. Bodyform[46]), a Tweet (Oreo[47]), a novel search term (comparethemarket.com),[48] an online action video,[49] a billboard that generates sales, shares and media content,[50] or even a TV spot,[51] all can define a brand, at least for a while. Even social ads can do so occasionally, but usually only when they garner coverage because of how bad they are, as in the late 2017 Dove[52] racism imbroglio. Media

content is read by audiences who understand it in the context of other media content. Intertextuality isn't a novel way to understand some ads' creative executions – it is the precondition for understanding how audiences read advertising. The ads are the paratextual trailers to a brand's unwritten story, but the audience never get to read the book, they piece together the story from their experience of its paratexts.

3. **Audiences, not consumers.** The point of an advertisement is to be seen and noticed, and preferably to be enjoyed. An ad that gives a moment's entertainment to someone who will never buy the advertised product or brand is not a wasted ad. Non-buyers define the cultural meaning of a brand just as much as consumers of it. What is more, when a lot of people enjoy a brand's advertising, more of them might consider buying it. How many of the millions of viewers who enjoyed Volvo's Epic Split video happened to be truck buyers for logistics companies? We don't actually know, but our guess is, not many. Some real-time tests found that truck buyers rated the ad less effective than more traditional b2b truck marketing, but, we think, advertising effectiveness tests often miss the point. Advertising that generates publicity has many side benefits. For example, corporate advertising that viewers enjoy makes the sales force's job easier – the dreaded cold call is less cold when there's a talking point to break the ice. There can also be an effect on other stakeholders that can generate a stronger sense of unity for the organisation when corporate advertising makes a splash. The Volvo CMO felt that the Epic Split campaign brought their marketing, PR, content and sales functions closer together.[53]

4. **Publicity to activation.** Advertising strategy entails a continuum from publicity to activation. Advertising is mediated communication – it is entertainment, information, publicity: it isn't personal selling. It can't answer objections to purchase (at least, not yet, because of the limitations of chatbots). But campaigns have to ensure that the publicity generated by advertising can be leveraged into sales by making it easy and convenient to find and buy the brand. Leaving aside issues of retail distribution, customer service, quality management, and so on, the activation end of the continuum for mediated communication lies mainly in the hybrid digital forms of advertising that combine the ad-like format with click-through buying capability. In other words, any consumer ad campaign has to have its search and social element at the spout of the sales funnel[54] set up optimally. People will Google the brand if they are interested (other search engines are available),

and it might be useful to remind people now and then with retargeted ads on social media. In general, we are sceptical of the value of forcing people to see ads – behavioural targeting works inasmuch as it makes it easier for someone to act on a pre-existing predisposition. Cookie-based programmatic ads don't have any psychological insight into users, they don't know if the user has a predisposition to buy. It is well documented that average overall CTRs for search and social are around 1%. That doesn't mean the 99% is wasted – after all, annoying as they may be, these ads are earning the brand a little oxygen, but the point is to understand how the activation continuum flows (the CX (customer journey) and UX (user experience)) in particular cases.

5. **Creativity – good advertising needs to be good.** There is a long-standing and wholly redundant argument in advertising that pits creativity and effectiveness on opposing planes. This speaks to the absurd idea that advertising is a sales medium. If it doesn't persuade a viewer that they have to buy the thing, now, then it's no good. The flaw in this reasoning is that advertising can't persuade anyone to do anything, because it is a mediated communication, dummy. It doesn't talk back to stymie your objections with sophistical logic, it doesn't negotiate. An ad can be persuasive in an indirect way in that it can present something in an attractive light, but this kind of persuasion is implicit. If audiences enjoy the communication, then an ad is doing a job. It has to be interesting/funny/gripping/evocative/striking and any other way you care to describe media content that's, well, good. Ad strategy is important in the sense that the client's marketing objective, the communication objective and the desired reaction from the audience ideally should be calculated. That might mean setting out to achieve positive publicity as an end in itself and setting up the marketing infrastructure support that can derive benefit from that.

We suggest that what our **CFAPC** acronym for paratextual advertising and branding strategy might be lacking in, well, memorability, coherence and alliteration, it makes up for in polysemic potential. We are considering marketing this book with competitions for the best mnemonic sentence – we'll start: Cute Friesians Angry at Piebald Cattle. Or perhaps change the order – our scheme is not sequential. Advertising Clichés Cannot Persist Forever. Entries on a postcard.

We accept that such a rubric suffers from all the usual failings, but we hope that each section is supported by detailed argument in the preceding chapters. The principles speak to a way of understanding advertising strategy that, we feel, is holistic, theoretically connected and logically coherent.

CONCLUDING COMMENTS

We have given over part of Chapter 7 to outlining the creative advertising development process as it evolved within the creative agency system, in order to understand how the best advertising was created before digitisation and media convergence. We then tried to nuance this process given the changes (and the existential threats) the creative ad agency system is facing. In particular, advertising strategy now has to be executed across multiple platforms and channels in single campaigns, and this, we suggest, is part of the reason why the traditional account team structure seems to be dissolving as the organising unit for advertising development. Teams are growing to accommodate all the cross-functional expertise that is now required, and this carries a risk of strategy drift. To try to address this, agencies have adopted initiatives such as losing a layer of management to focus on creative and/or tearing down office walls to encourage cross-functional dialogue, with varying success. The end point is that ad agencies are having to address the loss of their cultural authority (to borrow Douglas Holt's term used about marketing). The trust, or perhaps blind faith, agencies need in order to act as strategic partners to clients and create their best work is increasingly difficult for them to elicit.

We have argued that the changes in the advertising landscape have been, and continue to be, profound, but we maintain that Big Data and AI-driven programmatic advertising do not resolve the question of which half of advertising expenditure is wasted. Indeed, we suggest that none of it is necessarily wasted, because the focus should be audiences, not targeted consumers. Finally, this chapter has offered a five-point practical rubric for paratextual advertising strategy development, the **CFAPC** model, as a whimsically framed but sincerely intended representation of what, in our view, are the major applied implications of our paratextual perspective.

NOTES

1. https://www.netimperative.com/2021/07/13/global-ad-spend-trends-12-6 -increase-as-countries-recover-from-pandemic/

2. See https://www.theguardian.com/media/2006/jan/17/guardianobituaries
    .advertising
3. For a video of tributes to Webster and some of his ads, see: https://www
    .youtube.com/watch?v=YX70c0HFQVg
4. See http://news.bbc.co.uk/1/hi/magazine/4602906.stm
5. The first author once interviewed several account team members (sepa-
    rately) at a top ad agency who had all worked on a very famous ad. Each of
    them asserted with confidence that the iconic ad was 'my' idea.
6. See Mahsa Ghaffari, Chris Hackley and Zoe Lee, Control, knowledge,
    and persuasive power in advertising creativity: An ethnographic practice
    theory approach. *Journal of Advertising*, 48(2) (2019) 242–249. DOI:
    10.1080/00913367.2019.1598310.
7. Such as the effectiveness case histories kept by the UK industry body the
    IPA (Institute for Practitioners in Advertising): https://ipa.co.uk/awards
    -events/effectiveness-awards/ease
8. Developments of this research were subsequently published in various
    journals including Chris Hackley, Silent running: Tacit, discursive and
    psychological aspects of management in a top UK advertising agency.
    British Journal of Management, 11(3) (2000) 239–254 (https://onlinelibrary
    .wiley.com/doi/abs/10.1111/1467-8551.00164). Chris Hackley and Arthur
    C. Kover, The trouble with creatives: Negotiating creative identity in adver-
    tising agencies. *International Journal of Advertising*, 26(1) (2007) 63–78.
    Chris Hackley, Account planning: Current agency perspectives on an adver-
    tising enigma. *Journal of Advertising Research*, 43(2) (2003) 235–246.
    Chris Hackley, From consumer insight to advertising strategy: The account
    planner's integrative role in creative advertising development. *Marketing
    Intelligence and Planning*, 21(7) (2003) 446–452.
9. A detailed account of the much maligned and much misunderstood account
    planning discipline in advertising does not fit here but interested readers can
    learn more from the website of the UK Account Planning Group: https://
    www.apg.org.uk. Merry Baskin gives a short but authoritative introduc-
    tion to the discipline's origins here: https://www.apg.org.uk/single-post/
    2001/04/02/what-is-account-planning-and-what-do-account-planners-do
    -exactly; and also see John Griffiths's resource: http://www.planningabov
    eandbeyond.com/planning-craft/out-of-the-box-thinking/stanley-pollitt/.
    Two of the most important books about account planning are John Griffiths
    and Tracey Follows, *98% Pure Potato* (2016), Penguin Books (https://www
    .penguin.co.uk/books/111/1111190/98--pure-potato/9781783522286.html)
    and Stanley Pollitt's, *Pollitt on Planning* (2000), NTC Publications (out of
    print).
10. Examples of published work from this line of research include Rungpaka
    Amy Hackley and Chris Hackley, Television product placement strategy
    in Thailand and the UK. *Asian Journal of Business Research*, 3(1) (2013).
    Available at: https://papers.ssrn.com/sol3/papers.cfm?abstract_id=2346385.
    Chris Hackley, Rungpaka Tiwsakul and Lutz Preuss, An ethical evaluation
    of product placement: A deceptive practice? *Business Ethics: A European
    Review*, 17(2) (2008) 109–120. DOI: 10.1111/j.1467-8608.2008.00525.x,

full text at: https://www.academia.edu/805055/An_ethical_evaluation _of_product_placement_a_deceptive_practice. Rungpaka Tiwsakul, Chris Hackley and Isabelle Szmigin, Explicit, non-integrated product placement in British television programmes. *International Journal of Advertising*, 24(1) (2005) 95–111. DOI: 10.1080/02650487.2005.11072906. The ideas are of course summarised in our Sage text, *Advertising and Promotion*.

11. Paul Grainge and Catherine Johnson, *Promotional Screen Industries* (2015), Routledge. https://ipa.co.uk/effworks/effworksglobal-2020/why-does-the -pedlar-sing

12. https://www.redbeecreative.com

13. https://www.redbeemedia.com

14. Mahsa Ghaffari, Chris Hackley and Zoe Lee, Control, knowledge, and persuasive power in advertising creativity: An ethnographic practice theory approach. *Journal of Advertising*, 48(2) (2019) 242–249. DOI: 10.1080/00913367.2019.1598310.

15. Chris Hackley, How divergent beliefs cause account team conflict. *International Journal of Advertising*, 22(3) (2003) 313–331. DOI: 10.1080/02650487.2003.11072856.

16. Artificial Intelligence machines are used in social media advertising to conduct real-time testing in order to compare the response to two variables in the copy of the ad or the imagery, and they are better at this than humans, thereby improving the CTRs or click-through rates of the ad. Of course, AI machines have to be programmed by humans with templates for the ad in the first place, so it is inaccurate to describe what they do as creative.

17. Byron Sharp, *How Brands Grow – What Marketers Don't Know* (2010), Oxford University Press.

18. Former BMP account planner Paul Feldwick in *Why Does the Pedlar Sing?*, published by Matador, with a video introduction here: https://ipa.co.uk/ effworks/effworksglobal-2020/why-does-the-pedlar-sing

19. We elaborate on this, with references to advertising theory review publications, in Chapters 2, 4 and 5.

20. Feldwick supports this with reference to data from the IPA Effectiveness Databank: https://www.marketingsociety.com/the-library/pursuit-effectiveness

21. https://everythingwhat.com/who-is-the-sun-newspaper-target-audience

22. https://everythingwhat.com/who-is-the-sun-newspaper-target-audience

23. According to one estimate: https://www.allsaintsacademydunstable.org/wp -content/uploads/2019/04/The-Sun-Fact-Sheet.pdf

24. https://www.thesun.co.uk/motors/12750527/rolls-royce-ghost-smooth -effortless-floats-along/

25. Chris Hackley and Rungpaka Amy Hackley, Advertising at the threshold: Paratextual promotion in the era of media convergence. *Marketing Theory*, 19(2) (2019) 195–215. DOI: 10.1177/1470593118787581.

26. Chloe Preece, Finola Kerrigan and Daragh O'reilly, License to assemble: theorizing brand longevity. *Journal of Consumer Research*, 46(2) (2019) 330–350. DOI: 10.1093/jcr/ucy076

27. Chris Hackley, *Marketing in Context: Setting the Scene* (2013), Palgrave Macmillan.   http://www.palgraveconnect.com/pc/doifinder/10.1057/9781137297112

28. https://www.theguardian.com/world/2017/oct/08/dove-apologises-for-ad-showing-black-woman-turning-into-white-one

29. https://yougov.co.uk/topics/consumer/articles-reports/2017/10/13/dove-brand-perception-suffers-advert-backlash-it-s

30. https://www.vccp.com/work/ctm/no-place-like-home

31. https://www.youtube.com/watch?v=TdyeNQnTmEY

32. https://www.youtube.com/watch?v=Y9znA_dwjHw

33. https://www.youtube.com/watch?v=-zOrV-5vh1A

34. For example, with regard to Sony Balls: https://www.thinkbox.tv/creative/behind-the-scenes-of-great-ads/sony---balls/

35. Google categorises content as Hero (entertainment), Hub (go-to platforms) and Help (need-driven information). We touch on this in Chapter 1 when mentioning Lazar Dzamic and Justin Kirby's excellent book, *The Definitive Guide to Strategic Content Marketing: Perspectives, Issues, Challenges and Solutions* (2019), Kogan Page.

36. https://econsultancy.com/why-brazil-bound-brands-should-be-wary-of-cultural-mistakes/

37. https://www.marketplace.org/2009/12/01/chinese-girls-just-not-barbie/

38. https://www.linkedin.com/pulse/smartphone-today-has-more-computing-power-than-nasas-1960-offermann

39. https://forsman.co/work/volvo-trucks/the-epic-split-feat-van-damme-live-test-6

40. https://en.wikipedia.org/wiki/The_Epic_Split

41. https://www.fastcompany.com/3031654/how-volvo-trucks-pulled-off-an-epic-split-and-a-game-changing-campaign

42. We should be so lucky.

43. It was once common for ad agencies to be paid commission on the media space they bought, rather than being paid for their work. Since media buying became outsourced to specialist media agencies this payment method has declined and agencies now bill clients for work using similar accounting techniques as lawyers or consultants.

44. For more on the term cultural intermediaries applied to ad agencies see Anne M. Cronin, Regimes of mediation: Advertising practitioners as cultural intermediaries? *Consumption Markets & Culture*, 7(4) (2004) 349–369. DOI: 10.1080/1025386042000316315.

45. In one of his expertly crafted pieces advertising his cultural branding consulting framework, a 2016 piece in *HBR*, Douglas Holt contrasts brand-produced content with influencer content to make the point that successful content is seen as entertainingly authentic (or authentically entertaining). We are fans of Holt's cultural branding, but we refer to axiom number 5 below – content doesn't have to be authentic, it just has to be good. Holt's piece is here: https://hbr.org/2016/03/branding-in-the-age-of-social-media

46. Bodyform responded to an amusing post from a man to amplify a conversation about periods, generating more than two million YouTube views for their video:

https://techcrunch.com/2012/10/21/how-bodyform-made-period-hell-funny
-on-facebook-and-clocked-up-more-than-two-million-youtube-views-in
-the-process/?guccounter=1&guce_referrer=aHR0cHM6Ly93d3cuZ29vZ
2xlLmNvbS8&guce_referrer_sig=AQAAALi2pA7q8TzbITfBqYsKWF
-96RVJw7tTSumi9mhuMMG06FXJRQfnNfks-RnjcEc39oRrBRugCG1
A1F6vi4uhO_b4GzawpgZl5zxBB086ZKqpKLqSIEQcGUkfj5rqvCP
f9mNJMSOQXVXuMHuvBHlH7LspeurYd57fu1XAl5g-uJku

47. A tweet during a blackout became the most liked ad of Superbowl 2013: https://www.wired.com/2013/02/oreo-twitter-super-bowl/
48. The award-winning campaign began with a brief to find a better search term than 'price comparison', 'market' or 'compare': https://www.theguardian .com/video-advertising/meerkat-mission
49. BMW's The Hire changed not only car marketing but the advertising industry as a whole as it showed how brands can create entertaining online video content that can reach larger audiences with greater impact than TV: https:// shots.net/news/view/how-bmws-the-hire-ushered-in-a-new-era
50. BA's The Magic of Flying campaign rewrote the possibilities for digitally enabled OOH (Out Of Home) advertising: https://www.campaignasia.com/ article/my-campaign-the-making-of-british-airways-the-magic-of-flying/ 468941
51. Contrary to conventional wisdom amongst digital acolytes, TV remains the most effective ad medium: https://www.thinkbox.tv/news-and-opinion/ newsroom/why-tv-remains-the-worlds-most-effective-advertising/
52. https://www.independent.co.uk/news/business/news/dove-unilever -personal-care-racism-advert-black-woman-white-a7988641.html
53. https://www.marketingmag.com.au/hubs-c/volvo-epic-split-roborgh/
54. https://lucklessdigital.com/digital-marketing-sales-funnel/

8. Paratextual advertising and the future

INTRODUCTION

In this book we have set out to rethink advertising as paratextual communication. In this, the final chapter, we will try to draw together the various threads to sum up what we think we mean by paratextual communication in advertising and branding, and to point to future directions for research and practice that are implied in our perspective. We begin by explaining why we think our humanities-based approach bridges disciplinary boundaries. We then revisit some of Genette's key principles for paratextuality in order to try to underline the basis for our approach. We end the chapter by saying a little about some of the many topics which we did not have space to discuss in this book but which, we feel, could be fruitful sites for paratextual analysis that builds on our approach.

PARATEXTUAL ADVERTISING – A CROSS-DISCIPLINARY APPROACH

Our approach might on occasion seem to conflate the categories of branding and advertising. We focus, though, on the deep overlap between the two. We consider that most advertising campaigns, not only for commercial goods and services but also for charities, political parties, health policies, and so forth, conform to the logic of branding, while the logic of consumer branding cannot be understood fully without thinking of advertising too. Consumer brands have material and legal assets, but these are matters of quality management, logistics, the supply chain, and so on. We focus on brands as phenomena of communication.

From a managerial perspective, we see paratextual branding as the superordinate activity into which advertising dovetails. By advertising, we mean any form of communication connected explicitly or implicitly to the brand. Finally, we have focused this book around the idea that the brand is the notional primary text into which its various advertising paratexts grant entry, so the two, branding and advertising, are inseparable in our scheme.

We have drawn on a selection of influences from academic research and practice which might be viewed as eclectic but which, we feel, have an underlying coherence. In particular, we draw on research-based ideas about advertising and consumption from the humanities and cultural anthropology, and we try to marry these (in the line of argument from Chapters 4 and 5 to Chapter 7) to managerial research. On the face of it, our literary influences might seem ill-fitting with, for example, Andrew Ehrenberg and colleagues' tradition of work, which is mainly quantitative with much store placed on statistical empirical generalisation. We also mention Byron Sharp who uses plenty of hard data sets to support his arguments on the relationship between advertising and market share. We feel, though, that our humanities perspective is not only consistent with the conclusions reached by these researchers, but that it also provides a richer and fuller explanation for the kinds of insights Ehrenberg and Sharp have generated from quantitative data sets. We feel that paratextual theory, while not being necessary to the conclusions we reach about advertising practice, helps to knit together the various themes in the field into a more coherent whole, giving shape to ostensibly divergent thinking in marketing, branding, communication and advertising theories.

We will now briefly revisit some of Genette's ideas that are central to our perspective, in order to try to underline the theoretical basis of our approach. We will then offer some tentative suggestions on the implications our approach might have, if any, for future practice and research that considers the ideas herein.

We have bandied about some literary concepts that we think are useful to our scheme, from those that are pretty well used in business school advertising research, such as intertextuality, to the frankly exotic, such as performative citationality. Our superficial treatment of complex ideas like Bahktin's dialogism, Iser's reader-response, Kristeva's aforementioned intertextuality, du Saussure's semiology, Barthes' mythology, and, indeed, Nakassis' performative citationality[1] might irk the theorists. Our aim, though, has not been to provide introductions to these fields[2] but, rather, to give due acknowledgement to the various traditions that we touch upon in our overall scheme. We hope that our cursory acknowledgement of these theoretical areas here will encourage readers new to literary analyses of advertising to pursue their own enquiries into areas of interest.

The way we have co-opted selected ideas from Genette's complex sub-categories of transtextuality, equally, deserves far more nuance and precision than we give them here. Our purpose is to try to broaden the use of Genette's ideas in the full range of business school advertising and related areas of study, and also to provide a basis for their use in advertising and branding practice. Overall, we want to show why the idea of paratextuality captures a powerful unity within the bewildering multiplicity of post-digital advertising communication, and offers a sweeping insight into the relationship between advertising communication and branding.

REVISITING GENETTE, PARATEXTUALITY AND ADVERTISING

Perhaps the most accessible account of Genette's fundamental ideas on the paratext is in his paper translated by Marie Maclean in 1991 for the *New Literary History* journal.[3] The paratext, to recap, is comprised of the peritexts that are contained within the material limits of the work, such as title, footnotes, cover blurb, and so forth, and the epitexts that surround the work but are exterior to it, such as advertisements, published reviews, and so on. Genette uses many sub-divisions of peritext and (especially) epitext to designate their spatial and temporal relation to the primary text. We will not dwell on these, partly because the sub-categories of paratext in electronic media would take an entire work to log, and partly because we are concerned mainly with the broad principles of the primary text – paratext relation. Genette describes the paratext variously as a threshold, a vestibule (referring to Borges) and an intermediate or undecided zone between the text and what lies outside it: '... a zone, not just of transition, but of *transaction*' (p. 261; original italics). The audience's experience of the transition will not necessarily be homogeneous or predictable, because it will be mediated by the reader response.

It may be an unfeasible cross-disciplinary leap, but it is hard not to think of anthropologist Victor Turner's work on liminal experience here[4] (also mentioned in Chapter 6). The paratext is not merely passive in cueing the reception of the text; in engagement with a reader it has the potential to transform the meaning of the reading, and of the work, through a transactional process that is mediated by the reader's interpretive vocabulary. The paratext is a threshold object with liminoid or ludic[5] potentialities for the transformation of experience and identity. The transformative element of paratexts seems to move them beyond the mere framing of the form or genre (whether the text is read as a novel, a poem, an advertisement) and into a more expansive and fluid realm of form allied with meaning. Genette goes on:

> The paratext thus is empirically composed of an assorted set of practices and discourses, of all sorts and of all ages, which I incorporate under this term in the name of a community of interest, or convergence of effects, which seems to me more important than their diversity of aspect. (P. 262)

Paratexts, to an extent, materialise the primary text. Genette maintains that a text cannot exist without its paratexts, while the converse is not so – paratexts can exist without texts, as in lost ancient works of which only the title, translations or commentaries remain.

Applying Genette's ideas on literary paratexts to the world of electronic texts, we might acknowledge that, in media-saturated, technologically advanced societies, paratexts are the principal textual form. Long-form media content still abounds, but the volume of short-form content is far greater because the audiences are greater. The tweet, the like or upvote, the photograph or short video, the vignette, the précis, the review, the two-paragraph news story, the social media comment or picture, the news headline: these are examples of what we mean by short-form content that lends itself to the universal activity of media browsing, and there is a distinctively paratextual character to this kind of incomplete, frag-mented content. With regard to the countless types of short-form branded media content that lie under layers of sponsorship and cross-promotion, mediated experience today is heavily weighted towards the consumption of short-form paratexts as opposed to longer engagement with primary texts, however that may be conceived.

The brand's meanings, then, are located within the space between a matrix of constantly shifting paratexts and the reader. One of the chief axioms we feel our paratextual perspective supports is that, counter to the dominant view in brand management wisdom, there is no brand 'soul' or 'essence' – there are distinctive assets, to use Sharp's term, but these can be an artefact of the advertising, they are not necessarily core to the brand itself, because, for the audience, there is no core. The brand asset might be an advertising jingle, a slogan, an image that serves for a time. As Melissa Aronczyk states,[6] a brand's 'boundaries are contingent on the exigencies of the paratext, and the text itself becomes subordinate to the paratext' (p. 113). The brand is an empty signifier or an 'undefined space' (p. 112) the purpose of which is to 'create signifieds for itself on an ongoing basis' (p. 112). The brand's signifieds arise from paratexts of all kinds, including advertising, broadly conceived as every possible type of brand exposure to audiences. These paratexts inscribe meanings into the ambiguous space of the brand. In effect, they write the brand story, together with the interpreting audience. This insight from paratextual theory invites a shift in perspective on advertising and brand management, and a shift in research approaches.

THE ANALYSIS OF ADVERTISING PARATEXTS

Genette suggested that a framework for the analysis of paratexts would need to consider a paratext's spatial, temporal, substantial, pragmatic and functional characteristics.[7] That is, where and when does the paratext appear and disappear? What material form does its existence take? To whom is it directed, and from whom? And, what is its purpose, and for whom? Such a direction of analysis could move us towards a taxonomy of paratextual advertising types, forms and, perhaps also, purposes. It is conceivable that a paratextual branding strategy might begin with an audit of existing brand paratexts, although this would be a static analysis with the limitations that implies, and not necessarily any more useful than the management strategy cliché of the environmental audit and strengths/ weaknesses analysis. Normative conclusions about what the direction of future travel ought to be cannot logically be derived from a static analysis of the current situation, but management theory deals with David Hume's is/ought problem by ignoring it.[8]

Nor do we suggest that it is possible to derive a science of interpretation from an analysis of brand paratexts and their reception. As we have stated throughout this book, our adaptation of Genette's ideas does not cohere with his apparently structuralist ontology, even though Genette's ideas appear not to cleave too closely to structuralist orthodoxy. As for strategy initiatives in marketing, these are invariably influenced by intuition, supposition, internal organisational politics, and trial and error, however detailed the justifications for them may be. This does not mean, though, that there is no value in an informed analysis of situations and scenarios. For pure research, there would be value in conducting such an analysis in order to backstop the sources and trajectories of brand meanings. With this in mind we offer a brief account here of the framework for brand paratextual analysis based on that which we provided in our *Marketing Theory* paper,[9] which in turn is adapted from Genette's principles. In the paper we used the comparethemarket.com meerkats case as a worked example, and we do so here.

The first step, then, in a brand paratextual analysis is to identify a para-text to begin the analysis, and we call this the originating paratext. The choice of originating paratext might be fairly arbitrary, but it could rep-resent a point of entry for the reader into the text. So, let us suppose that the first time a reader happens on the comparethemarket.com meerkats is through an encounter with the hard copy of the book published in 2010 entitled *A Simples Life: The Life and Times of Aleksandr Orlov.* Perhaps a person was searching an online bookseller for a gift for their child, and this book appeared in the search.

Following Genette's principles, we establish the temporal, spatial, substantive and pragmatic characteristics of the book. The originating paratext in our example appeared about a year after the launch of the first TV spots and quickly rose to the top of the UK best-sellers lists. It retains a presence on bookselling websites and in archived press coverage.[10] The temporal characteristics influence whether the book would be a prior epi-textual paratext, encountered before the reader had heard of the meerkats or their linked brand, thereby providing a threshold into the brand, or one encountered after others had been encountered, thereby acting as an inner threshold into a new or adjusted meaning of the brand for the reader. The spatial, substantive and pragmatic characteristics of the book were, respectively: (a) that it occupied shelf space in bookshops at the time of release, it was stocked by online retailers, and was advertised by the pub-lisher; (b) that the book was categorised as a celebrity autobiography and printed on good-quality paper, richly illustrated with portraits of Orlov and his extended family, along with an audio version; and (c) that the book was written with mock earnestness in the stilted English Orlov uses in the TV ads, and the name of the human ghostwriter does not appear in the credits. comparethemarket.com is named as the copyright owner and author. The book is dictated by the demanding and impatient Orlov to his long-suffering assistant, Sergei. The reader (at least, the adult reader) is assumed to understand that the book is a fiction, and this fact operates as a silent intertext, as it does in all the elements of the Orlov family storyworld (extending to a TV soap opera, a website and various filmed vignettes). The silence of the intertext, we suggest, operates to enhance, rather than diminish, the promotional effect.

The distal function of the brand paratext is to advertise the brand. The proximate function is to entertain a wide audience that conspires in the joke pretence that Orlov and his family are real. The various paratextual products of this campaign are parodic para-epitexts that work to mutually reinforce the effect of all the connected paratexts. The book as paratext intersects intertextually and comedically with the literary genre of the celebrity biography. According to Anthony Patterson and colleagues,[11] it also includes elements of the literary genres of comedy and adventure, while referencing Hollywood movies and other TV ads.

The anthropomorphic use of the meerkat intertextually references a UK BBC TV nature show that aired between 2005 and 2008 called Meerkat Manor.[12] The popular show[13] provided a very endearing characterisation of the animal, creating a presence for the animal in popular culture, as Chris Miles and Yasmin Ibrahim's[14] work explains. Incidentally, it may be useful to note that an Australian brand used the meerkats as a motif and failed, suggesting that the endearing image of the cute creature is not enough in and of itself to explain the success of the use of it in the UK campaign. However, the popularity of the creature around the world may be an important variable – in France, for example, the comparethemarket. com brand uses ferrets, not meerkats, in its promotion.[15]

There are, clearly, many intertextual trajectories that could be derived from the book, not limited to the social media likes, shares and comments. The book generated much media coverage as the industry and mainstream press were keen to exploit the cult status of the campaign by getting in on the joke in parodic book reviews. The media, branding and advertising trade press wrote up admiring accounts of the way the campaign elevated the brand from a moribund state to number one in a sector that as a whole was boosted by the campaign. The ultimate triumph of the VCCP agency is that in executing their brief to create a novel search term for the brand, they created many more: not only 'meerkats' or Aleksandr Orlov but Meerkovo (the meerkats fictional home region in Eastern Europe), their home, Meerkat Manor, and all the other characters in the family.

The meerkats are a special case, but they are a useful way of illustrating what we think is the rich potential of paratextual brand analysis as a source of insight into brand paratextual dynamics that might inform strategy, in addition to being a rudimentary basis for pure research conducted from intellectual curiosity. The establishment and emergence of brand meaning in consumer culture is not a mystery – it derives largely from mediated paratexts. We suggest that mapping the connected dynamics of a brand's paratexts within a wider media landscape could be a basis for research into brand analysis, advertising effect and consumer cultural meaning. In his book *Show Sold Separately*, Jonathan Gray[16] states that '... paratextual study not only promises to tell us how a text creates meaning for its consumers, it also promises to tell us how a text creates meaning in popular culture and society more generally' (p. 26). It is to this wider issue that we now turn.

ADVERTISING PARATEXTS AND CONSUMER IDEOLOGY

Paratextual advertisements lie at the nexus of brand promotion and consumer ideology. We have not focused on the ideological character of paratextual advertising, because that would be another book, but we have made the point that much of it takes the form of implicit promotion that is designed to valorise and normalise the presence of brands and consumption practices in every life. The suggestive juxtaposition of brands with successful, happy, beautiful people in advertising is part of the ideological apparatus of a consumption-driven society. The mechanisms of paratextual advertising are powerfully ideological, in the small 'i' sense of implicitly supporting interests, values and social relations that are not explicitly stated. The old definitions of traditional advertising usually state that the advertising message is placed on a paid-for advertising medium, it originates from an identifiable source and it is aimed at achieving an identifiable purpose. A great deal of paratextual advertising strategically fudges the origin, the purpose and the ultimate sponsor of a piece of media content, or, at least, fails to make these matters explicit.

For example, a video clip of a basketball game might include the visual identifiers of many brands on the athletes' uniforms, on court-side banners and hoardings and on the clothes of spectators, and the clip might later appear within or alongside other content on video sharing websites, news or sports media footage, with screen-captured images appearing on other social media platforms, shared by fans. In this way, the motives, identity and message of brand owners are rendered indistinct, unlike the brand itself which appears at the heart of one of society's most powerful and widely viewed ritual events – sporting competition. We have provided many examples of brand-sponsored paratexts the source of which remain unclear, partly because epitextual brand content might in some circumstances have greater source credibility than that which clearly is paid for and produced by and for the brand.

The inherently ideological character of brands, and their communication, has not escaped the attention of socio-cultural brand writers and researchers. For example, Douglas Holt and Douglas Cameron averred that brands can be understood as myths informed by ideologies.[17] The beliefs and associations that circulate around brands cannot necessarily be said to correspond with the observable truth because a brand image is seldom expressed solely as a series of statements of fact. Rather, brand meaning is a cultural construction, perpetually reconstituted through its paratexts and open to vague interpretations. When Edward Bernays[18] coined the term Public Relations (aka PR) as a euphemism for the commercial propaganda he practised, he saw advertising and propaganda, well, PR, as different entities. Bernays felt that advertising, by the narrow, traditional definition, was a weak force of persuasion, while official media, news, information and entertainment were far more influential. Bernays used news media to powerful effect in his campaigns for many clients. Today, the rise of digital platforms has eroded the distinction between advertising, news and entertainment when these are viewed over social media. Movie product placement was once thought unethical because it is advertising that pretends to be entertainment[19] – few would make that point today, as the distinction between editorial and advertising is lost on many consumers.

Today, for many media audiences, there is only content, and all content is available as an ideological vehicle to advertise brands. Officially produced news, entertainment and information and content produced ostensibly by private 'users' now occupy the same, intimately interconnected, space. A focus on paratexts not only reveals the propagandistic character of contemporary advertising under digital media convergence, but also locates the understanding of media paratexts at the centre of pressing debates about democracy, citizen education and online misinformation.

We do not suggest that brands that use paratextual advertising are necessarily unethical. Advertising had always had an ideological character. What we suggest is that the reach of media ideology is wider and more penetrating than ever before, and the spaces occupied by brands are also occupied by those with party political and other motives. A critical understanding of media texts has never been more important as a part of a liberal education. Paratextuality is an important route into a better understanding of how media texts wield their influence.

CONCLUDING COMMENTS

In the concluding chapter we have reiterated the basics of Genette's paratextual theory as we have adapted it to advertising to move towards an analytical framework for understanding how advertising paratexts exert their influence on audiences. We have hinted at the broad, cross-disciplinary potential for future research into advertising and media paratexts, and we concluded with some comments about the broader media context for paratextual analysis as advertising content converges with political, ideological and propagandistic media content. Our book is about advertising, as we conceive it in the broadest possible terms as any form of communication that connects with brands. But it is not just about advertising. It is also about thinking critically about marketing, media and management. We hope that our account of advertising contributes to an enhanced understanding of media and to a broadened critical and liberal arts approach to business and management scholarship and education. We feel that such an approach is important not only to the advancement of management theory and practice, but also to a wider critical understanding of how ideas flow through media content.

NOTES

1. See Constantine V. Nakassis, Brand, citationality, performativity. *American Anthropologist*, 114(4) (2012) 624–638. DOI: 10.1111/j.1548-1433.2012.0 1511.x.
2. Please see some of the many sources we cite for introductions to these areas.
3. Gérard Genette and Marie Maclean, Introduction to the paratext. *New Literary History*, 22(2) (1991) 261–272. DOI: 10.2307/469037.
4. Victor Turner, *The Ritual Process: Structure and Anti-Structure* (2017; first published 1969), Routledge.
5. See Chris Hackley, Rungpaka Amy Hackley and Dina H. Bassiouni, Imaginary futures: Liminoid advertising and consumer identity. *Journal of Marketing Communications*, 27(3) (2021) 269–283. DOI: 10.1080/13527266.2019.1694564.
6. See Melissa Aronczyk, Portal or police? The limits of promotional paratexts. *Critical Studies in Media Communication*, 34(2) (2017) 111–119. DOI: 10.1080/15295036.2017.1289545.
7. Gérard Genette and Marie Maclean, Introduction to the paratext. *New Literary History*, 22(2) (1991) 261–272, 263. DOI: 10.2307/469037.
8. For an introduction to Hume's is/ought problem, see: https://en.wikipedia .org/wiki/Is%E2%80%93ought_problem
9. Chris Hackley and Rungpaka Amy Hackley, Advertising at the threshold: Paratextual promotion in the era of media convergence. *Marketing Theory*, 19(2) (2019) 195–215. DOI: 10.1177/1470593118787581.
10. https://www.prnewswire.com/news-releases/meerkat-memoir-hits-no-1 -spot-in-celebrity-autobiography-battle-111341974.html
11. Anthony Patterson, Yusra Khogeer and Julia Hodgson, How to create an influential anthropomorphic mascot: Literary musings on marketing, make-believe, and meerkats. *Journal of Marketing Management*, 29(1–2) (2013) 69–85. DOI: 10.1080/0267257X.2012.759992.
12. Meerkat Manor, BBC 2: https://www.bbc.co.uk/programmes/b00812sw
13. https://en.wikipedia.org/wiki/Meerkat_Manor

14. Chris Miles and Yasmin Ibrahim, Deconstructing the meerkat: Fabular anthropomorphism, popular culture, and the market. *Journal of Marketing Management*, 29(15–16) (2013) 1862–1880. DOI: 10.1080/0267257X.2013.803142.

15. https://www.thisismoney.co.uk/money/news/article-2817052/BGL-boss -Matthew-Donaldson-mission-shake-insurance-market.html

16. Jonathan Gray, *Show Sold Separately: Promos, Spoilers, and Other Media Paratexts* (2010), New York University Press.

17. Douglas Holt and Douglas Cameron, *Cultural Strategy: Using Innovative Ideologies to Build Breakthrough Brands* (2010), Oxford University Press.

18. Here is a short, accessible piece by Richard Gunderman, by way of introduction to Bernays and his work: https://theconversation.com/the-manipulation -of-the-american-mind-edward-bernays-and-the-birth-of-public-relations -44393

19. On the ethics of product placement: Chris Hackley, Rungpaka Amy Hackley and Lutz Preuss, An ethical evaluation of product placement: A deceptive practice? *Business Ethics: A European Review*, 17(2) (2008) 109–120. https://onlinelibrary.wiley.com/doi/10.1111/j.1467-8608.2008.00525.x

Index

Printed and bound by CPI Group (UK) Ltd, Croydon, CR0 4YY

16/04/2025